SOUNDING RIGHT

Robbins Burling

NEWBURY HOUSE PUBLISHERS, INC.
ROWLEY, MASSACHUSETTS 01969
ROWLEY • LONDON • TOKYO

1982

Library of Congress Cataloging in Publication Data

Burling, Robbins.
  Sounding right.

  Bibliography: p.
  Summary: Examines ways in which one learns a
second language and outlines methods to hasten
this process.
    1. Languages, Modern--Study and teaching.
[1. Languages, Modern--Study and teaching]
I. Title.
PB35.B795   418'.007   82-2211
ISBN 0-88377-216-7   AACR2

NEWBURY HOUSE PUBLISHERS, INC.

Language Science
Language Teaching
Language Learning

ROWLEY, MASSACHUSETTS 01969
ROWLEY ● LONDON ● TOKYO

First printing: October 1982

Printed in the U.S.A.   5   4   3   2   1

Preface

This book grew from both love and frustration: love of speaking with people in their own language; frustration at doing it so very badly.

At one time or another I must have tried—or been subjected to—every method ever devised for learning a language. I was exposed to high school Latin by the tried and true but deadly tedious grammar-translation method. In both high school and college, French was presented to me in a form that can only be described as "modified eclectic" and that, among other things, required interminable memorization of irregular verbs. Later, when pedagogical fashion changed, I flirted briefly with Chinese, and endured equally interminable pattern drills. I also engaged in a variety of desperate attempts at self-help when I found myself surrounded by people with whom I passionately wanted to talk.

The most lasting result of all these long years of struggle is the conviction that there must surely be a better way of going about it. For, in spite of every effort, I never seemed able to achieve the kind of easy fluency that I craved. Something was missing. Three times during long visits abroad I watched in awe as my children mastered subtleties that escaped me, and on more occasions than I care to count I watched with suppressed annoyance as Sibyl, my wife, accomplished feats with language that somehow passed me by.

Sibyl and I, in fact, have worked out a cooperative routine, one version of which goes something like this: We enter a shop together and, having practiced my three hundred words of Burmese or my twenty words of Greek, I confidently toss off a convincing phrase or two. With a bit of phonetic facility and more than a bit of foolhardiness I persuade the man behind the counter that I can handle his language. He then responds in rolling, but mysterious cadences. Through the mush of foreign noise I imagine that I catch a crucial word or two and so I venture another phrase. Sibyl, who up to now has been standing quietly to one side, says, "No, Rob, he didn't say that." She then proceeds to explain what he really did say so that I can work out a more appropriate response. Our strange three-way conversation proceeds until our errand is complete. I do the talking; she does the understanding. Here is a pathology of language not yet listed in the literature of speech correction.

What do I do wrong? Why do I, like so many Americans, find it so difficult to learn another language? When we go to live in foreign parts I set about with eager resolution to build my linguistic skills. I read; I study grammar; I practice; I work out rules; I analyze. I study the patterns of phonological alternation, and I work out ingenious rules that demonstrate the underlying logic of surface irregularities. I delight in the wonderful patterns of this wonderful language. But somehow I never seem to know what they are saying to me.

Sibyl will not be bothered with the linguistic wonders. A morphological rule bores her, and a phonological rule dismays her. She will listen to the language, however, and she will read, and, in a quiet way that has been mysterious to me, she learns. The truth is, that she has always learned languages more successfully than I. I have felt that she is a trifle timid about speaking, but she does better in the long run. I can only conclude that my valiant, linguistically inspired efforts have been almost entirely misdirected.

Finally, in what now seems like a long overdue assertion of common sense, I had to conclude that I had always gone wrong by trying to say too much too soon. I too readily accepted the unstated but pervasive assumption that "learning a language" and "learning to speak a language" are synonymous. I thought I had to *say* things in order to get them lodged properly in my mind, so I sought out occasions when I could *use* my language—that is, *speak* it. Language, I imagined, is behavior; behavior needs practice, practice makes perfect. So along with my linguistic analysis I practiced. But I did not learn quickly enough to avoid embarrassing my children with my mistakes. In the heat of conversation the fancy rules were of little help, and the other person never said what those painfully memorized dialogues had led me to expect.

Sibyl and our children let the language flow over them. They absorbed it. They said little at first, but when they knew enough they spoke, and when they spoke they spoke well. They spoke because they had things to say, not because they were seeking out occasions for practice. I struggled to talk before I had an adequate knowledge of the language, and the result was perpetual frustration. I finally came to believe that language instruction ought to be radically reoriented so that we would first help students to understand. Only later—after they have learned enough of the language to manage it without embarrassment—should we encourage them to say anything at all.

I began to think more seriously about language instruction and about the unstated assumptions that provide the underpinnings of our conventional methods. Many of these assumptions began to seem dubious to me and, as I abandoned them, a number of attractive alternatives began to seem plausible. With one unorthodox method I tried to help people learn to read French, and later I joined several colleagues in developing an equally unorthodox method for helping people gain an aural comprehension of Indonesian.

I also happily discovered that I was not alone in thinking about the desirability of emphasizing comprehension. A scattering of free spirits around the country, and around the world—Asher, Gary, Nord, Postovsky, Winitz and others, whose work is referred to repeatedly in the following pages—had been thinking along similar lines. I have profited from their ideas and their experiences, and taken comfort in their agreement, even when some of my colleagues closer to home remained skeptical. I also found my way to the literature on child language and on second language learning, and to the rapidly developing, overlapping field of child second language learning that has, I believe, a special relevance for foreign language pedagogy. And, finally, I have tried to draw these strands together in this book.

I begin by reviewing a number of assumptions that seem to pervade the field of foreign language teaching but that should, I believe, be seriously questioned. Once questioned, radical methods of helping people learn foreign languages suddenly become plausible. I then review those aspects of child language acquisition, particularly child second language acquisition, that seem to be relevant for older learners. Having made an abstract case for putting comprehension first, I go on in Chapters 3 and 4 to review two programs in which I have participated, one a method of teaching reading, the other a method of teaching comprehension of the spoken language. These are not intended to be definitive descriptions of fully tested techniques, but rather suggestions about the kinds of experiments that become possible once one is liberated from the productive bias of most formal language instruction. In Chapters 5 and 6 I offer a number of less detailed suggestions about other possible ways of helping students understand, and I conclude with a few more general remarks about the nature of language and language learning.

Perhaps I should warn the reader that I am not much of an experimentalist. Before I became a linguist I was a field anthropologist, and I have always felt more at home with a single well-rounded case study than with a mass of statistics telling me more than I care to know about a few almost trivial facts. I have learned more about language by watching my wife understand shopkeepers than by counting errors made by experimental and control groups on carefully constructed "instruments." I admire controlled experiments, and I understand the need for trying out new teaching materials in carefully controlled circumstances, but I also see deep problems in many of these experiments. The number of variables that ought to be controlled is so vast that genuine comparability usually eludes us. Differences in student background, aptitude, and motivation, differences in teacher skill, and the excitement of the experimental situation itself are only the most obvious variables that have to be controlled before any certain claim can be made about the superiority of one method over another. More often than we sometimes recognize, our experimental designs impose such simplistic measures of achievement that the rich complexity of language, and the wealth and variety of its use, are surrendered in exchange for a quite trivial "reliability." The arguments and conclusions I offer in this book, therefore, depend more on intuition and experience, and less on experiment and measurement, than is typical of the recent literature on second language acquisition. I offer as many anecdotes as experimental results.

In addition to the debt I owe my wife and my children for their frequent help, I am more conventionally indebted to several helpful organizations and to many colleagues, friends, and students. Chapter 3 is an adaptation of a more complete description of my French program, published as: "An Introductory Course in Reading French," *Language Learning*, Vol. 28, No. 1, pp. 105–128, 1978. I am indebted to the Center for Research on Learning and Teaching at the University of Michigan, which provided a modest grant that allowed me to hire a research assistant to help me prepare materials. As the assistant, Norma Ware did a wonderful job in organizing and cleaning up my manuscript in preparation for its first full-scale trial. I am also much in debt to Professor Raymonde Carroll of the Romance Languages Department for her generous assistance and her consistent encouragement, to Professor Michio P. Hagiwara who paved the way for me to try out the materials in class, and to Jacqueline Rosten who, with grace and good spirit, presided over the class.

The experiment in machine-aided aural instruction in Indonesian was a joint effort, guided by my old friend and long-time collaborator A. L. Becker and myself, but with the essential participation of many others, including Joyce N. Tomasowa, Frances Hays, and Fred Lupke. Patricia B. Henry, in addition to devoting hours to designing lessons and teaching classes, wielded her pen to produce the wonderful sketches we gave our students, including those reproduced in Chapter 4. We received warm support from the Language Laboratory of the University of Michigan, in particular from its director, Erwin Hamson, and from Barry Legien, an inventive genius of a technician who devoted hundreds of hours designing, building and maintaining our equipment. The project was given modest but crucial initial support by the Center for Research on Learning and Teaching and the Center for South and Southeast Asian Studies at the University of Michigan. More lavish funding then came from the Office of Education of the Department of Health, Education, and Welfare.

My trip to Sweden was sponsored by the Socialantropologiska Institutionen of Göteborgs Universitet where I spent the year 1979–80 as Guest Professor. Of the many people who helped me in Göteborg, I am particularly indebted to Staffan Hellberg and Anders-Börje Andersson who, over the course of the year, helped me toward some understanding of what was going on in my head as I struggled to learn their language. Nancy Hansen offered me generous, high spirited, and essential help with the preparation of the diagrams.

More generally, I am indebted to many of my friends, students, and colleagues at the University of Michigan who, through the years, have helped me clarify my views. Sometimes they have agreed with me; sometimes, they have thrown my own ideas into sharp relief by their contrasting ideas, always they have helped me. In addition to those already mentioned, I single out especially several members of the Linguistics Department—Deborah Keller-Cohen, John M. Lawler, and Larry Selinker. To all of them, my thanks.

Acknowledgments

The author would like to express his appreciation for permission to quote several passages from other works: To MIT Press and to Edward Arnold Limited for the passage from *Linguistics and Language Teaching* by David A. Wilkins on page 6; To John Wiley and Sons for the rules of French taken from *L'Echelle* by R. L. Politzer, M. P. Hagiwara, and Jean R. Carduner on page 14; To Longman Group Limited for the rules of English taken from *A Communicative Grammar of English* by G. Leech and J. Svartvik on pages 9–10. Chapter 3, "Reading a Mixed Language," is an adaptation of an article, "An Introductory Course in Reading French" that first appeared in *Language Learning,* Vol. 28, pags 105–28, 1978. The portions of this article that are reprinted here are reproduced with permission of the editor of *Language Learning.* Patricia Henry has graciously permitted her sketches for Indonesian lessons to be reproduced here on pages 73, 74, and 76.

Contents

1

Some Enduring Pedagogical Assumptions

Enrollment in foreign language classes in American high schools and universities rose steadily until it reached a peak about 1968: 3,518,413 foreign language enrollments in high schools and 1,073,097 in colleges and universities. After that year enrollment began a gentle decline. High school registrations coasted downward to 3,048,331 in 1978, almost half a million off the total ten years earlier, while by 1977 college and university enrollments had gone down to 883,222, a loss of about 190,000 in nine years (Morrison, 1977; Hammond and Scebold, 1980).

These fairly modest declines assume more significance once we realize that total enrollment in both high schools and colleges was still rising during the same period, so that the percentage of students studying foreign languages dropped rather more sharply: from 27.7 percent of high school students in 1968 to 21.9 percent in 1978, and from 15.5 percent of college students in 1968 to a mere 8.9 percent in 1977. Anyone who regards the ability to use a foreign language either as an essential component of a liberal education or as a practical necessity for life in a shrinking world, is likely to view these figures with some alarm. They seem to suggest a renewed isolationism. They are an indication of an all too widespread American ethnocentrism.

On the other hand, when one considers what a small proportion of these student millions either enjoy their encounter with a foreign language or acquire any useful ability to speak or read, one must also be impressed by the persistent high level of enrollment. In both high schools and colleges enrollment is concentrated at the elementary level. Many students drop after a single year, and only a small number go on to a third or fourth year. This high attrition suggests (even if we did not already know through abundant personal reports) that most language classes are not

1

much fun, and surely no one would claim that two years in an American language classroom can be expected to confer much useful linguistic skill on any appreciable number of students. For most of the four million foreign language students in American high schools and colleges, the time spent in the foreign language classroom is time wasted.

It is possible, in other words, to read the enrollment figures in two sharply contrasting ways. They suggest a scary tendency of Americans to turn away from the rest of the world; they also suggest the enormity of our foreign language instruction industry. It grinds relentlessly but rather futilely along. It occupies hour upon hour of the time of tens of thousands of teachers and millions of students, but its visible accomplishments are hard to find. Most Americans remain dismally monolingual. Those few who do acquire a useful command of a foreign language rarely do so through the typical stages of our formal educational system. That foreign language instruction survives at all, in the face of its manifest failure to reach any discernible goal, is testimony to the high importance that Americans place on foreign languages. In spite of all past failures we always seem willing to try again.

It is the gap between the acknowledged importance of foreign languages and our meager results that explains the restless search for new methods. For language pedagogy has always been even more susceptible to fashion and fad than other fields of American education. Perceptive foreign language teachers have been able to see, even more clearly than the rest of us, just how few of their charges emerge from their classrooms with any useful amount of the language under their caps. The result has been that teachers (and those who take it upon themselves to advise teachers) have been restlessly driven to search for a better way. The grammar-translation method yields to the direct approach. The direct approach is replaced by the audiolingual technique which was supposed to work such miracles during the Second World War. Techniques with names like "the play way," "counseling-learning," "suggestopedia," and now "the cognitive method," each have their day of promise. But as each of these once new programs turns out to be less than stunningly successful in the ordinary high school or college classroom, teachers turn to still other techniques or to renamed and recycled fads that promise greater success. (Close, 1977, offers an irreverent review of changing fashions in language teaching.)

Throughout these changing fashions, however, there have endured a number of assumptions about language and language teaching. Occasionally one or another assumption is explicitly asserted or defended or, more rarely, attacked, but more often these assumptions are simply taken for granted. They form a part of the unquestioned invisible context within which the enterprise of foreign language instruction grinds along. If we are to clear the air and open up language instruction to more radically unconventional methods, we have to ferret out as many of these unconscious assumptions as we can. Once made explicit, some will seem questionable, and, as seen in the following pages, I am sufficiently skeptical to be ready to try methods that violate them. More specifically I want to discuss, and cast doubt on, eight assumptions that strike me as characteristic of most American language pedagogy in the last three or four decades. Each of the eight needs discussion.

1. *All aspects of a language are interdependent.* Most language teachers, like most linguists, take it for granted that all aspects of a language (its phonology, syntax, and lexicon, for instance) are closely interrelated and interdependent. Phonology is expressed through words; words are organized into phrases and sentences by syntactic rules; syntactic rules are related in many complex and wonderful ways to phonological rules. All the weight of tradition in linguistics encourages the search for these interrelationships. Dictionaries, grammars, and phonological descriptions may sometimes be bound in separate covers, but every linguist agrees that no description of a language can really be complete without attention to all its aspects.

More delicately, the assumption of interrelatedness extends to the relationships among various aspects of grammar or among various aspects of phonology or vocabulary. The nouns of a language can hardly be well understood except when compared and contrasted with the verbs. The tense system of verbs interrelates with the adverbial system. The phonological changes undergone by a noun as it passes through its various declensional forms can be expected to show parallels with the changes undergone by a conjugating verb. The distinctive features of consonants must have some sort of relationship with the distinctive features of vowels. The organization of meaning of kinship terms must be related to the meaning found in pronouns. And so forth.

These claims are certainly correct. All these interrelationships are there to be seen and heard. Nevertheless, when we carry our interest in these interrelationships into the foreign language classroom, we bring ourselves grief. A language comes to be seen as such a complex and delicate mechanism that it is difficult to teach anything at all without teaching everything else at the same time. In the very first lesson of almost every foreign language class, students are expected to learn the meaning of a few words, enough about pronunciation to mouth these words, and enough about syntax to tie them together in some sort of conventional order. A student needs to know an awful lot just to say a tiny bit.

In reality, a person can learn a vast amount about some aspects of a language even while neglecting its other aspects. A few people manage to master the syntax and lexicon of a foreign language while making virtually no concessions to its phonology. They speak with rich and remarkable foreign accents, but handle the rest of the language with easy fluency. These speakers demonstrate that all aspects of a language do not have to be learned simultaneously after all.

Under the right circumstances it can also happen that massive doses of the lexicon from one language can be used without its grammar. In some parts of the world where English is widely used as a second language today, especially where it is the language of education and learning, speakers feel free to incorporate into their own language virtually any English word they think will be understood (Burling, 1970:77). Lexicon, like phonology, can be used independently of the rest of language.

Of course we want our students to learn the entire language, but the parts of a language are not so tightly interdependent that it is either necessary or reasonable to try to teach them all at once. Perhaps we could start with lexicon, wait a bit for syntax, and wait even longer for phonology. Or at least we ought to be willing to consider quite radical revisions of the conventional order of presentation in foreign language instruction. We should not assume too easily that anything like the traditional order is inevitable.

2. *Languages do not mix.* Along with the assumption of interdependent parts, we hold to a reciprocal assumption that different languages occupy such different worlds that they never can, or never should, be mixed. Perhaps our distaste for mixing languages is an aesthetic matter. We admire the beauty of "pure"

French or the vigor of "pure" English. But if we imagine that languages *cannot* be mixed, we are simply wrong. It is far easier to mix them than to keep them "pure." Did anyone ever study a language without producing such playful nonsense as *Je ne want pas to study pour un other minute*, or *I have noch nicht meine breakfast ge-eaten?* Usually we ignore such efforts. They seem to be nothing but the frivolous antics of schoolchildren, but frivolous or not, they show clearly just how easily languages can be mixed. All linguistic borrowing, in fact, gives testimony to the eternal permeability of linguistic boundaries.

Nevertheless, when teaching foreign languages, we have obstinately discouraged mixing. Our students hardly need to be told not to mix their vocabulary, but we struggle desperately to prevent them from showing the influence of their native language either in the form of a foreign accent or in the form of syntactical interference. Later I will suggest that we can devise some exceedingly helpful language lessons by ignoring the injunction against mixing languages. Students mix them anyway. We can exploit their ability to do so.

3. *Grammar and phonology, being more central to language than the lexicon, have a corresponding priority in instruction.* Even while assuming that all aspects of a language are interrelated, we have often acted on the apparently contradictory notion that syntax and phonology form the core of a language, and that they deserve first attention in early foreign language instruction. Vocabulary, by this assumption, is relatively superficial, and some suppose that it takes care of itself rather easily once the grammatical core is mastered. Charles C. Fries, for instance, said, "In learning a new language . . . the chief problem is not at first that of learning vocabulary items. It is, first, the mastery of the sound system—to understand the stream of speech, to hear the distinctive sound features and to approximate their production. It is, second, the mastery of the features of arrangement that constitute the structure of the language" (Fries, 1945:3). Of course, students need a few words from the very start, but the bulk of vocabulary has often been seen as posing relatively few problems for the learner, and has even been seen as a bit of a distraction until more important matters are first taken in hand.

This downplaying of vocabulary is supported by the habits of many linguists. Many of us have delighted in the patterns of phonology and syntax but have had few ideas about how to handle the more loosely structured lexicon, or those aspects of meaning with which the lexicon is most closely tied. Thus it was probably inevitable that when linguists began to make their influence felt among language teachers, they would encourage attention to the structural features that interested them while playing down the importance of the lexicon and of meaning.* With the help and encouragement of linguists, elaborate phonological and syntactic drills were devised. Subtle contrastive studies of the sounds of the native and foreign languages have led to ingenious schemes for helping students overcome the muscular habits of their own languages. Elaborate (and deadly) pattern drills were produced in the hope that they would help students learn, and then overlearn, the new syntactic patterns.

In a work that represented itself as describing the "linguistic method," Politzer and Staubach (1961) went the whole way. They suggested that it might be possible ". . . to eliminate meaning almost totally from the initial phases of language instruction. It is entirely possible to teach the major patterns of a foreign language without letting the student know what he is saying" (Politzer and Staubach, 1961:18). These intrepid researchers do admit that there might be some problem in keeping "the student's motivation and attention alive during the drill period," hardly a frivolous worry since the type of course they envisaged ". . . consists necessarily of several months of uninterrupted pattern drills and mechanical stimulus-response manipulations" (P. 19).

---

*D. A. Wilkins states the situation clearly in summarizing what he takes to be the dominant tendency of recent language pedagogy: ". . . linguists characteristically view language as a structured system, and their preoccupation has been almost entirely with those aspects of language whose structure is most susceptible to scientific analysis—phonology and grammar. Linguists have had remarkably little to say about vocabulary and one can find very few studies which could be of any practical interest for language teachers. Reflecting the linguist's concern with grammar and the related view that mastery of a foreign language depends upon complete control of its grammatical rules, we find the methodologist's emphasis on the subordination of vocabulary teaching to grammar teaching. The range of vocabulary, we are told, should be deliberately restricted while grammar is still being acquired so that the learner's powers of acquisition can be concentrated on what is most important. To spend time at this stage learning vocabulary is to be diverted from the true context of language acquisition. Once the pupil knows the many grammatical frames, then to expand the number of words which can operate in the frames is a relatively simple task. It therefore comes later" (Wilkins, 1972a:109). Wilkins then goes on to describe his own quite different view of the importance of vocabulary.

Is it possible to imagine a more dismal way to learn a language? I would like to believe that Politzer's and Staubach's students rose in furious rebellion against such a dehumanized undertaking, but I fear that they merely dropped the course in quiet resignation, convinced of their own lack of aptitude but swelling the statistics of those who begin a language without ever reaching a useful level.

To most people, the important thing about language has always been its meaning. The structure of a language is merely a tool by which to convey the meaning, and, except to a few grammarians, the less time spent worrying about structure the better. Let's get on to the message! Every foreign language student who manages to survive the paradigms or pattern drills and to move past the elementary stages knows that her real struggle is to learn the meaning of all those words. Hundreds of words! Thousands of words! And, one is tempted to intone, "millions and billions and trillions of words!" Their meaning has to be learned before one can read with any degree of skill or pleasure and before one can either speak or understand. It is simply false to imagine that words come easily once the "grammatical core" of the language is mastered. Rather, as I will argue in Chapter 6, the grammatical "core" will come more easily if a good many words are learned first. (See Macnamara, 1972, and Schlesinger, 1968, who argue for the priority of meaning over syntax in decoding.)

It is largely in the lexicon of a language that meaning is lodged. To use a language in any useful way it is necessary to know a great many words; but, as I argue in Chapter 6, it is possible to understand a vast amount, and even to say a great deal, with no more than the most rudimentary control of grammar. Pidgin languages manage to be useful precisely because their speakers are willing to learn and to use a good many words while avoiding anguish over grammatical niceties or phonological conformity.

I believe that overemphasis on phonological and syntactical details, an emphasis that has too often been encouraged by linguists, has brought nothing but grief to generations of students. They would have done better to get on with the meaningful vocabulary that leads to practical communication.

4. *Adult learners cannot rely on unconscious acquisitional processes but must be given explicit instruction, particularly in grammar.* An impressive body of literature grew up in the sixties and seventies which sought to demonstrate that children pass

through a critical age when language learning is easiest. After the critical age, the natural ability to acquire language was supposed to decline. A few observers went so far as to follow Chomsky's usage (1965) by speaking of some sort of "Language Acquisition Device" (e.g., McNeill, 1970). As soon as this was abbreviated to LAD it seemed very nearly to have become an organ of the body, like the big toe or the gall bladder. Some time around puberty, the child's LAD was supposed to decay so that anyone older than about fourteen who was rash enough to try to learn a language was well advised to get some explicit instruction. The language would no longer come naturally, as it would to a child. (See Krashen, 1975, for a sympathetic but judicious review of this evidence.) These ideas have been given prestigious support by neurologists and neurolinguists (Penfield and Roberts, 1959; Lenneberg, 1967; Lamendella, 1977), and some have specifically recommended that language instruction begin while the preadolescent plasticity of the brain still allows language to be readily learned (Whitaker, 1978).

More recently the idea of a critical period for language learning has come under strong criticism. I review some aspects of this controversy in the next chapter. Now it is enough to insist that the ability to acquire linguistic patterns unconsciously, without having them explicitly formulated and taught, cannot possibly come to an abrupt or total end at puberty. A few adults, after all, do manage to master the syntax of a foreign language. Since no one has yet come close to providing an explicit description of the full syntax of any language, there is no conceivable way that an adult, any more than a child, could possibly gain all her knowledge through explicit instruction. Anyone, adult or child, who gains a firm control of a language simply must acquire some of it through unconscious acquisitional processes. The point ought to be obvious, and I am hardly the first to assert it (cf., Selinker, 1972; Chomsky, 1969). Nevertheless, textbook writers and language teachers sometimes act as if everything needs to be taught explicitly, as if nothing can be left for the student to absorb unconsciously.

After decades of criticism of the grammar-translation method it is strange to have to charge textbook writers with providing more explicit grammatical description and instruction than desirable. The objection to the grammar-translation method was always that it offered the student too many rules and treated the language as an abstract puzzle instead of as a natural living thing. But formal rules seem to be abandoned only to rise in a new guise. The audiolingual pattern practices may not have been accompanied by explicit grammatical rules, but they were designed in the clear belief that students had to be drilled, minimal step by minimal step, in a systematically progressing path through the various patterns of the language. Even if not laid out as formal rules, the patterns were, in principle, supposed to drill students in everything they would need to know.

As each new linguistic fashion emerges, it is reflected in new ideas about new things we have to teach. Shortly after transformations became a center of linguistic research, they appeared at the center of pattern practice. More recently, linguists have given increasing attention to things called by such terms as "communicative competence," "pragmatics," or "style shifting," and faithful attempts are now being made to instruct students in such matters. Language teachers even worry about making sure that students acquire both "competence" and "performance" (e.g., Chastain, 1976:160). All these efforts are examples of the apparently insatiable urge to provide deliberate instruction in every facet of language that anyone investigates, and to trust nothing to natural absorption.

Let me support this claim with an example. As a spin-off from a genuinely important enterprise, *A Grammar of Contemporary English* by Randolf Quirk et al. (1972), two of the co-authors, Geoffrey Leech and Jan Svartvik, produced a shorter version entitled *A Communicative Grammar of English* (1975). According to the Preface, this abridgment ". . . is intended primarily for the fairly advanced student [of English as a foreign language], for example the first-year university student" (p. 10). The book is divided into 886 numbered sections, most of which consist of detailed descriptions of the subtleties of English. Many, in fact, are so subtle that few native speakers have any conscious awareness of them. In conformity with modern notions, these include details about styles—formal and informal, written and spoken, polite and familiar—as well as careful statements about intonation, e.g.:

41
A RISING tone, on the other hand, expresses 'uncertainty' or 'incompleteness' or 'dependence'. A *yes-no* question (*see* 778) usually has a rising tone, as the speaker is uncertain of the truth of what he is asking about:
    [Are you léaving?]   [Can I hélp you?]

Parenthetical and subsidiary information in a statement is also often spoken with a rising tone, because this information is incomplete, being dependent for its full understanding on the main assertion:

If you *líke*, we can go for a *pìc*nic *láter*. (p. 39)

The bulk of the book, however, deals with syntax. It is difficult, in a short space, to give a feeling for its treatment of syntax, but section 417, "Given and New Information," is fairly typical.

Given and new information
417
We can roughly divide the information in a message into GIVEN INFORMA-TION (something which the speaker assumes the hearer knows about already) and NEW INFORMATION (which the speaker does not assume the hearer knows about already). In [8] above, 'He was speaking' is given information: it is already given by the preceding clause; in [10], 'you see him' is given information for the same reason:

He was speaking   to *mè*   *If*   you sée him . . .

GIVEN   NEW   NEW   GIVEN

As new information is obviously what is most important in a message, it receives the information focus (*ie* nucleus), whereas old information does not. Naturally, personal pronouns and other substitute words, because they refer to something already mentioned or understood, normally count as old information.

Note
Notice that given information and new information are what the speaker *presents* as given and new respectively. What *in fact* the hearer knows or assumes may be a different thing. For example, a speaker might say:

(Margaret likes Picasso), [but Jane *hàtes* modern painting.]

The position of the nucleus here means that the speaker assumes that the hearer knows that Picasso is a modern painter. But of course, the hearer might not have heard of Picasso, or might not regard him as a modern painter. (pp. 172–173)

The scholarship represented in this book is impeccable. It fairly bulges with thoughtful description of English. Its rules are even stated with reasonable clarity. I can imagine an occasional student, at just the right instant in his education, being helped by one or another of its sections. But I can much more easily imagine the great majority of students being simply overwhelmed by the terrible mountain of detail placed in their hands: details that look like injunctions; details which no native speaker uses conscious-ly; details that the foreigner is somehow expected to understand and to act upon before he will be counted as knowing English.

The intricate rules offered by *A Communicative Grammar of English* are worse than useless. They convey a sense that speaking a language is like grinding through a problem. Language becomes a massive quasi-mathematical game in which one must simultaneously juggle a thousand simultaneous equations just to produce a single proper sentence. The book represents a reincarnation of ancient grammar-translation methods dressed up with modern terminology that gives it an aura of linguistic sophistication. As a linguistic exercise it is fine; as a pedagogical tool it is a disaster.

Now I do not wish to deny a place for explicit grammatical rules, or to suggest that adults should be abandoned as fully to their intuitive processes as children. Adults surely have abilities that infants lack, and the ability to profit from an explicit generalization is certainly one of them. We can quickly chop through masses of difficulty by offering an appropriate generalization as a summary guide to the way a language works. Even translation can save an enormous amount of time. An infant must sometimes struggle for months before finally sorting out the contrasting meanings of words such as "yesterday" and "tomorrow." Happily, adult students and foreign language teachers can cut this struggle short by a quick translation. But it is a delusion to imagine that all the patterns of a language can be learned in this way, and most language courses suffer from far too many explicit rules. Our challenge is not to provide a detailed description of every aspect of the target language, as books like *A Communicative Grammar of English* seem to suggest, but rather to encourage and exploit, to the fullest extent possible, the intuitive, even unconscious, abilities that all people possess that allow them to absorb the patterns of the language naturally.

5. *The "four skills" should be taught together.* The assumption that speaking, understanding, reading, and writing should all be taught together is often implicit, and from time to time it surfaces as an explicit precept, as for instance in Kenneth Chastain's general book, *Developing Second-Language Skills* (1976). Chastain repeatedly asserts the desirability of working on all four skills, and he has separate chapters on each. Most language pedagogy reflects this view.

But why? Many students will surely find some skills more useful than others. Almost everyone will find some value in knowing how to read, but only a small minority will ever want to write anything in the foreign language. Since written mistakes show up with such dreadful clarity, writing is also a far more difficult skill than reading. Thus there seem to be excellent reasons for limiting serious attention to writing to the minority of advanced students who have specialized interests. Some students need to read but will never have any desire to carry on a conversation, and a four-skills approach may simply slow down their progress and make it more difficult for them to reach their pragmatic goal. Different students have different needs, and there is no good reason to force them all to work in lockstep.

To this it may be objected that the four skills support one another. Learning to write helps with reading, reading helps to build vocabulary, and this, in turn, helps when embarking upon a conversation. Of course, there is a kernel of truth in this claim, but the amount of extra anguish required to keep errors below the threshold of embarrassment in writing is hardly likely to yield as much return toward the goal of reading as the same amount of effort spent pleasantly with a novel. Let's be skeptical of the four-skills doctrine.

6. *The spoken language has priority over the written language.* There is no rule that all implicit assumptions must be logically compatible, and it is a bit of a contradiction to the belief in the four-skills approach that many language teachers have taken it for granted that the spoken language comes first. This idea is supported by the valid observation that children learn to speak before they learn to read, and by the ideas of an older generation of linguists who looked upon writing as a "secondary symbolism" dependent on, and derivative of, the spoken language. It may seem obvious that the "natural" sequence of language learning proceeds from the spoken language to the written language.

It ought to be somewhat embarrassing to proponents of this view that people really do sometimes learn to read foreign languages without learning to use them orally. Listening and speaking may help with reading, but reading may also help with listening and speaking. A clear priority in a course for adults who are already literate in their own language is not, after all, obvious.

Some experimental energy has been directed toward determining whether verbal learning proceeds more rapidly and efficiently through visual or auditory channels, but the research is fraught with difficulties, and the conclusions are by no means clear. Impressionistically, however, it is difficult to avoid the suspicion that by the time people reach college age, the written language has assumed such importance that students may actually find it difficult to separate the spoken and written language. They may even feel that the written language is the "real" language, and they may feel disoriented if denied the support of writing.

The question of whether visual or auditory learning should have priority for adults will not soon be settled, but we should certainly be skeptical of any insistence, based on a dubious analogy with infants, that the spoken language must always come first. Perhaps individuals vary. In the absence of firm knowledge, our best course is probably to provide materials that can be used flexibly enough to adapt to different goals and learning styles.

7. *Production should be at least as advanced as reception.* A good deal of lip service is paid to the desirability of training in all four skills, but when dealing with the spoken language, production has a way of sneaking into predominance. Except for a few rare early voices in the wilderness (e.g., Scherer, 1950, 1952; Ehrmann, 1963), and a number of important recent experiments (see below), it has been the virtually universal expectation that production—talking—must progress simultaneously with or even ahead of reception—listening. It is the central thesis of this book that this expectation is wrong.

In the next chapter I review the lessons we can draw from watching children as they learn languages. I must anticipate this discussion here merely to point to the common observation that children's comprehension is always in advance of their productive ability. (But see p. 39 where a different view is considered.) I suggest that we have failed to draw the obvious moral from this observation—that initial concentration on comprehension might be just as desirable for adults.

The presumption that production must go along with, or even be in advance of, comprehension is so pervasive that it is rarely even noticed, but one need only examine any random collection of introductory foreign language texts to see where the emphasis lies. It may be supposed that students will understand a memorized dialogue but the effort of memorization is directed toward production, and the judgment of success is based on production. All pattern drills, phonological and syntactic, are, of course, exercises in production. When students memorize vocabulary they usually put more effort into remembering how to express a meaning than how to recognize a word, simply because expression is harder than recognition. Translation into the foreign language is more difficult than translation *from* the foreign language, and it tends to be taken more seriously.

The grammatical generalizations offered by foreign language texts are usually productive rules. They tell the students how to organize words into sentences, or how to choose the proper suffix for a verb. Rules that tell learners what to look for or listen for in the new language, or how to interpret what they see or hear in a sentence, are far less common. Students are more likely to be told how to select the correct tense for a given situation than how to decide what time period is indicated by a tense they encounter.

As one example of productive rules, chosen virtually at random, consider two consecutive generalizations set out with admirable clarity in a standard introductory French textbook, *L'Échelle*, by Politzer, Hagiwara, and Carduner (1966), p. 241.

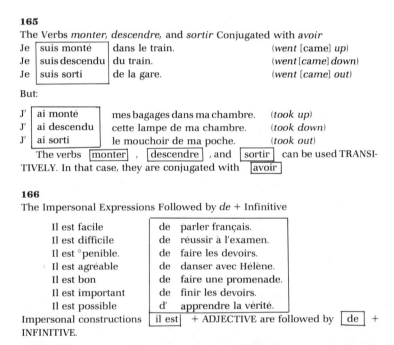

165

The Verbs *monter, descendre,* and *sortir* Conjugated with *avoir*

Je	suis monté	dans le train.	(went [came] up)
Je	suis descendu	du train.	(went [came] down)
Je	suis sorti	de la gare.	(went [came] out)

But:

J'	ai monté	mes bagages dans ma chambre.	(took up)
J'	ai descendu	cette lampe de ma chambre.	(took down)
J'	ai sorti	le mouchoir de ma poche.	(took out)

The verbs monter , descendre , and sortir can be used TRANSITIVELY. In that case, they are conjugated with avoir

166

The Impersonal Expressions Followed by *de* + Infinitive

Il est facile	de	parler français.
Il est difficile	de	réussir à l'examen.
Il est °penible.	de	faire les devoirs.
Il est agréable	de	danser avec Hélène.
Il est bon	de	faire une promenade.
Il est important	de	finir les devoirs.
Il est possible	d'	apprendre la vérité.

Impersonal constructions il est + ADJECTIVE are followed by de + INFINITIVE.

Rule 165 tells the student when to use *avoir* with these verbs. It is a guide to *use,* not a guide to understanding. To help one *understand* the language, the rule could be given as follows: "When you encounter *monter, descendre,* or *sortir* conjugated with *avoir,* you will know that it is being used transitively." The rule might not be necessary, however, since the context, especially the set of noun phrases that follows the verb, would usually show clearly whether or not the verb is transitive.

The generalization of Rule 166 would be even less necessary for students whose first goal is comprehension. At most it might be stated that "*de* will sometimes be encountered in places where the students' English habits lead them to expect nothing at all."

It might be argued that I am quibbling, that my reformulation of these rules is a minor matter. I would reply, however, that the cumulative impact of hundreds of such rules is by no means minor, for rules of this sort carry with them the unstated assumption that learning a language is primarily a matter of learning to speak (or to write), an assumption I believe to be quite wrong. It might also be argued that my reformulation of these generalizations as comprehension rules leaves them incomplete. My phrasing of Rule 166 will not help students decide when to use *de* and when to leave it out—but it is not supposed to. I suggest instead that when comprehension becomes sufficiently advanced, the *de* will come to "sound right" in this construction. The formal rule would never need to be stated at all, even at a later stage when the students begin to talk. They would use *de* because it sounds right, not because they have struggled with and remembered a formal rule. Second language learners could acquire an intuitive feeling for this rule without ever coping with it explicitly. That, after all, is how native speakers manage such rules.

Anyone inclined to remain skeptical of my charge that production has dominated foreign language instruction should inspect a randomly selected textbook and ask what proportion of the grammatical generalizations and rules found there are necessary (or even helpful) for a student who *only* wants to understand. I think the conclusion will be that the proportion is very small.

Of course, there are exceptions. A few books that offer specific help with reading are laid out in a way that is intended to guide reception, but these are hardly typical texts. Serious help with understanding the spoken language is unusual. Even books with such promising titles as *Improving Aural Comprehension* (Morley,

1972) and *Listening Dictation* (Morley, 1976) deal with a remarkably restricted kind of comprehension. Students are given isolated sentences to listen to. They are required to look for specific bits of information in these sentences, but the listening is often diluted by being combined with repetition and writing. Students do not learn to use, and they cannot take advantage of, the kinds of contextual clues that real situations always provide, and the more typical comprehension problems involved in listening to and getting the drift of extended discourse are not even approached. It is almost as if the problems of comprehension finally come down to such matters as discriminating *forty* from *fourteen*.

The widespread focus on production is not clearly recognized by the students and teachers who use the textbooks, and it is probably not even clearly recognized by those who write them. This is simply the way foreign language has always been taught. The pedagogical bias toward production reflects a similar bias in much of linguistics. More often than they realize, linguists phrase their grammatical generalizations productively rather than interpretively. Generative grammarians often assert that their rules are "neutral as between speaker and hearer," but they are more easily interpreted as modeling the activities of a speaker than those of a hearer. They are rules that, like the rules of most pedagogical grammars, tell us how sentences are formed, not how they are to be taken apart and interpreted. The result of lack of attention to aural comprehension is painfully obvious. It has been repeatedly observed that even students who perform very well in formal classes often have acute difficulty when they finally try to engage in real conversation, simply because they cannot understand (e.g., Belasco, 1971a, 1971b).

I see several reasons for the emphasis on production. First, production is much more easily studied. We know more about how the mouth works than about how the ear works. It is easy to listen to what people say; it is more difficult to know what, if anything, they have understood. Thus, it is hardly surprising that linguists have so often tended to organize their materials in a productive mode.

Perhaps it is inevitable that linguists have also encouraged language teachers to emphasize production, but language teachers have had plenty of reasons of their own. For language teachers also find it easier to deal with production. When students react to a foreign language, it is difficult to be certain whether or not they have really understood, but let them open their mouths to talk or take pen in hand to write, and the teacher can immediately judge their progress. Their errors stand out with dismal clarity. Thus, it is always easier for a teacher to test production than to test comprehension, and since both the students and their teacher anticipate tests of production, it is difficult for them to avoid concentrating on production in class and in homework. I suggest that this emphasis on production drastically distorts the language learning process.*

We should, after all, sympathize with students who are asked to produce language from the beginning of their studies. They cannot fathom any good reason why some sequences of words are allowed while others are forbidden. They will be bedeviled with the messy and senseless irregularities that occupy the heart of most languages. They cannot possibly avoid making mistakes. In most classrooms they will also be barraged by the mistakes of their classmates, and they will reinforce each other's errors. They will continually be frustrated by their slow progress and by their inability to converse on topics of interest, or to find the word they need to convey their ideas. They will have to expend great conscious effort on the structure of the language—to think about its sounds and its grammar—and this diverts their efforts from the area that is always most important to the fluent speaker—the meaning.

Receptive learners can avoid many of these problems. They need not be embarrassed by their own mistakes, and they need not be subjected to the mistakes of their classmates. They waste far less energy worrying about messy irregularities. Not having to recall words or constructions for active use they can make much more rapid and satisfying progress. When they finally begin to talk, they will do so on the foundation of an extensive knowledge

---

*In the last few years a number of radical experiments have been carried out in which the emphasis has been shifted to comprehension. Pioneering experiments in comprehension instruction were carried out by Valerian Postovsky at the Defense Language Institute at Monterey, California (1970, 1974, 1975, 1977) but a growing number of other scholars have been contributing their ideas: Asher, 1966, 1969, 1977; Winitz and Reeds, 1975; Reeds, Winitz, and García, 1977; Ingram, Nord, and Dragt, 1975; Gary, 1974, 1975, 1978; Swaffar and Woodruff, 1978; Davies, 1976, 1980; Snow, 1979; Majhanovic, 1979; Winitz (ed.), 1981a. The common goal of these experiments is to help students gain some initial ability to comprehend, in the expectation that production will come more easily afterward.

of the language. They will know words, constructions, and even sounds, and they will be able to avoid using incorrect forms because they will sense that they "do not sound right." They will have less need for abstract rules of grammar.

Once we wrench ourselves away from the pervasive assumption that production is central to language learning, a rich new range of possible pedagogical approaches presents itself. Some of these possibilities will be explored in later chapters.

8. *Language is behavior.* Production is easier to study and to test than comprehension, but there is an even more fundamental reason for the productive bias in our foreign language classrooms. We have suffered under the notion that language is merely a kind of "behavior" and that, like riding a bicycle or playing the violin, practice in the form of active, visible, muscular movement is essential for one who would learn.

A good deal of the linguistics of an earlier era was explicitly behavioristic. In spite of the many changes that have come to the field, behaviorist assumptions are by no means dead, and they survive with particular vigor in the area of language pedagogy. People, after all, move their muscles when they talk. They do behave. Perhaps first language learning is like walking, a skill for which we are naturally endowed, but a skill that still needs muscular drill and fine tuning to perfect. Second language learning, on the other hand, may be imagined to be more like swimming, a less natural skill than walking, and a skill that, unless learned very early, profits from deliberate guidance and instruction. If language learning is like walking or swimming, then it is clearly important to get the learners onto their feet and into the water. They must exercise their tongues and their lips in new ways. They must talk. Only practice will make perfect. To a long generation of linguists, and to the long generation of language teachers who have looked to linguists and behavioral psychologists for guidance, it has seemed obvious that trying to learn a language without practice in speaking would be absurd. (My characterization of the behaviorist view owes much to Postovsky, 1974, 1975a.)

All our phonological and syntactic pattern drills, all our memorized dialogues, all our insistence upon getting students to talk can only be understood as stemming from the belief that language is behavior. This insistence on the behavioral aspects of language is what makes early language instruction so grimly tedious. We offer rules, patterns, repetitions, incremental drills, and overlearning, when we should be offering the wealth, the humanity, and the meaning of language.

For language is also knowledge, and to reduce language to mere behavior is to dehumanize this most human of our abilities. When we emphasize comprehension, we emphasize knowledge. The learner's effort must always be directed toward extracting the meaning of what he hears and reads. Of course the student must listen to the new language through a confusion of unfamiliar sounds and syntax and read it through a morass of unfamiliar spelling, but these are relatively minor problems for a listener or reader compared to the problems they pose for a speaker. They fade part way into the background and gradually come to seem natural—to "sound right." What listeners and readers need are words—words and their meanings. For students who focus on comprehension first, learning need not be a mechanical drill to instill a new behavior; it can be an intellectual challenge to engage their interest. Mechanical drill is useful for conditioning rodents. Human beings deserve more.

Of course, our students will not be satisfied with understanding alone. They will also want to talk. But it is my thesis that talking will come more easily after understanding is well advanced. It is, indeed, my claim that no one should be obliged to say anything at all before she knows the language.

But this implies a radically altered conception of what it is to "know" a language.

As soon as we shake ourselves free from unquestioning acceptance of the eight assumptions reviewed, a number of unconventional techniques to help people learn a language will become apparent. I feel strongly that these eight assumptions should be abandoned, and in later chapters I offer some specific methods that violate them and that should make language learning both more rapid and more pleasant.

There are other issues for which the evidence strikes me as inconclusive, however, so the only judicious course is to keep an open mind. What, for instance, is the most effective balance between written and spoken language? I have admitted my skepticism about the "natural" priority of the spoken language, but I hardly think we have any clear idea of the optimum balance, for adults, between listening and reading. Perhaps individuals differ, and the best policy may be to look for techniques that are sufficiently flexible to meet differing needs and temperaments.

There is also room for disagreement about the relevance, for adults, of child language learning. If, when designing programs for adults, we can afford to ignore the childhood priority of spoken language over reading, we must certainly ask whether we should take seriously any of the evidence of children. The next chapter surveys some aspects of children's language learning, but there is room for much disagreement about its relevance for adults. There is always a danger that we will take seriously only those features of child learning that seem to fit our preconceptions, while rejecting the evidence as irrelevant when our preconceptions are violated.

Finally, a third area of disagreement is how much description of linguistic patterns and rules should be made explicit to adult students and how much should be left to unconscious absorption. I believe most foreign language instruction relies too heavily on explicit rules. An emphasis on comprehension would help relieve students of some of the burden of formalities, but I would never suggest that adult learners be denied all grammatical generalizations. Their ability to understand linguistic generalizations is an important advantage for adults, and it would be nonsense not to exploit it. However, the question of just how much formal grammatical description to offer adult students is likely to remain, for some time, more a matter of art and hunch, than of logic or science.

I will return to these questions in later chapters.

The Evidence of Children

We have all watched the magical way in which children learn to speak. The dismal results of second language instruction stand in unhappy contrast. Can we learn anything by watching our children?

The relevance of child language for adult foreign language pedagogy can hardly be accepted uncritically, and we should, in fact, view infant abilities with more skepticism than they usually evoke. A five-year-old who is ready for her first day of kindergarten shows a marvelous ease with language, but the discouraged adult learner must be tempted to believe that if he had few responsibilities, free room and board, and every chance to try out his developing language on interesting contemporaries, he too could reach the kindergarten level after five years. By then he might even have gained enough specialized vocabulary to be able to talk on some subjects that quite escape the kindergarten child.

What is surely far more awe-inspiring than infant first language learning is the achievement of the ten-year-old child who is dragged abroad by peripatetic parents and who, in a mere ten months, reaches a higher level of linguistic skill than she reached in her first language after five full years. Think of the difference between the child and her professorial father who spends his sabbatical year in France. In September the child finds herself swimming in the language of a French schoolroom and confined to French-speaking playmates, but well before the following June she speaks with such easy grace that no more than the faintest influence of English is still detectable in her French. At a time when her frustrated parents must still screw up their courage to attempt the modest linguistic challenge of asking for a half kilo of lamb chops, the child begins to wince at her father's mistaken genders. Like generations of immigrants to America, the adults may have to rely upon their school-aged children as interpreters. How do the children do it?

The child's lessons are likely to begin when she is thrown, nervously but decisively, into a French school. She may understand little at first, but she watches the other children, and she imitates them. The teacher directs the pupils to open their books. The foreigner looks sideways to see what is happening, and opens her book to the same page. The teacher makes a noise, the children get up and put on their coats, and so does the foreign child. The children go to the playground and the foreigner stands a bit foolishly on one side, but the children push her into position and force her to follow the rules of the game as best she can. For hour after hour, week after week, she is subjected to this kind of insistent involvement with the language and with the events with which the language is used. For several weeks, or even months, she may say very little except for set phrases like "*bon jour, madame,*" which are insistently impressed upon her, but she absorbs and absorbs and absorbs.

Meanwhile, what is her father doing? Visiting museums perhaps, talking in English with his wife, seeking out colleagues who speak English—even other Americans. He reads the Paris Herald Tribune and writes letters and an article in English. If he is unusually conscientious he goes three times each week to the Alliance Française for his French lesson where he is told to memorize the conjugations of irregular verbs and to write little exercises. He may try desperately to talk, but every time he opens his mouth he hears mistakes. He is embarrassed and frustrated. Those who hear him take pity on him. If they know any English at all they use it. By the end of the year the child is interpreting for her father.*

The achievement of ten- and twelve-year-olds is not only more impressive than that of infants, but also far more relevant for linguistic pedagogy. Older children, after all, share many of the advantages and disadvantages of adults. Older children can probably get hints about how the new language works from their experience with their earlier language. They should be able to exploit the same kinds of shortcuts that adults use by having words explained quickly by translation, rather than having to extract meaning laboriously from context. Like adults, older

---

*I speak with some feeling about the American child in France, for my description is drawn from the experience of my ten-year-old daughter. I deny, however, that my caricature of the American professor reflects my own behavior, except for the sorry truth that my daughter winced at my incorrect genders.

children surely have a clear general understanding of the uses to which language can be put and a broad semantic experience to which the language can be related. They have probably learned something about how to learn. (For a more extensive discussion of the advantages of older children, see Ervin-Tripp, 1974.) At the same time, the first language can be a source of interference for child second language learners, just as it is often a source of interference for adults. The recent flowering of child second language studies invites us to consider the experience of older child language learners and to ask why they so often seem to be so much more successful than adults.

Maturation

For reasons that I find a bit mysterious, but that may have something to do with misplaced awe of biological jargon, it has been more fashionable in recent years to attribute the differences in linguistic achievements of adults and children to physical maturation, than to the different social opportunities they have for learning. Following the appearance of Eric Lenneberg's *Biological Foundations of Language* (1967), it was especially popular to point to neurological changes, in particular to the "lateralization" of the brain, thought to occur at about the time of puberty. These changes have been blamed for putting barriers in the way of older children or adults who try to learn a language. If something decisive happens at puberty, then there may be a critical period before puberty during which language acquisition proceeds easily, and it is unreasonable to expect those who have passed this age to learn language by the same methods or with the same degree of success as younger children (Whitaker, 1978; Lamendella, 1977).

There is unquestionably great appeal in attributing adult difficulties to the inevitable result of physical and neurological maturation. It seems to explain the difficulties that post-pubertal learners so often have, and it offers great solace to frustrated adults dissatisfied with their accomplishments. If their brains have changed, it is hardly their fault.

Nevertheless, the hypothesis that neurological changes bring an end to a "critical period" for language learning has run into a number of challenges. Lenneberg's argument depended heavily on the evidence of patients with aphasia, evidence that is always difficult to interpret, and his specific attention to lateralization now seems questionable (Krashen, 1973). It has also been argued that the problems posed by the passing of the critical age are largely or entirely limited to phonology (Scovel, 1969), or that different aspects of language are actually subject to different critical ages (Seliger, 1978).

In addition to this apparent weakening of the critical period hypothesis, a few observers have pointed out that whatever difficulties adults have may be due to a quite different set of causes than the neurological one: the superior social opportunities that are typically available to adults (Ausubel, 1964; Neufeld, 1979; Schumann, 1978a; Burling, 1981). Children and adults, after all, are not treated in the same way, and they face very different expectations and demands. Their differing responses may be due as much to these differing opportunities as to their differing talents. In defiance of the enthusiasm for neurological explanations, a few brave voices have always argued that, under proper conditions, adults do not do so badly with language learning, so the "explanations" for adult disabilities may be explanations for something that does not exist, or that is at least much less severe than is often assumed.

It is not even as clear as many have assumed that preadolescent children always learn so easily. Our faith in the ability of children seems to be based on the experiences of children from reasonably high-status families who, like the professor's daughter just described, live abroad with their parents. These are children who receive confident encouragement both from their own families and from the speakers of their new language. They are readily and warmly welcomed into the community of their contemporaries, so they have easy access to the new language. Such children sometimes do spectacularly well. Those who have dealt with immigrant children in Sweden in the last decade, however, typically draw quite different conclusions about the ability of children. There, the common wisdom is that children go through great trauma as they try to cope with Swedish. Some are said to sit in school for several years without gaining an adequate command of the classroom language (Skutnabb-Kangas and Toukomaa, 1976). The problem seems to be that these are children from working-class families who speak low-status immigrant languages. These children are not always welcomed into a community of Swedish-speaking children and, if they have any effective participation with children of their own age, it is often with children who speak their own immigrant language.*

It may be that children learn more rapidly than adults when, as quite often, they have better social opportunities for easy access to the language, but when they are denied these opportunities, they face the same barriers as adults. For children, as for adults, access to and acceptance by a community of speakers is essential if a language is to be effectively learned in the absence of instruction. This fact is far more clear than the widely accepted idea that the passing of a critical period is to blame for adult failure. It is, therefore, important to explore the obvious alternative explanation for the apparent success of children: the ease with which they find encouraging social opportunities for language learning. The social setting, after all, is considerably more susceptible to manipulation than is the nervous system.**

Classroom and Naturalistic Settings

If we are to sort through the differences between older children and adults, it is essential to distinguish carefully between two contrasting settings in which language is learned: the classroom setting and what, for want of a better term, we can call the "naturalistic" setting. By "naturalistic" I mean the situation in

*The story is also told, however, of the Yugoslav child who sat mutely in class for several years without much sign of progress in Swedish. He was subsequently discovered to have learned a substantial amount of Finnish from the group of neighborhood children who were willing to accept him.

**The importance of the setting strikes me as so obvious and so overwhelming that I can only look with wonder at its neglect in the literature. Lamendella (1977), for instance, carefully distinguishes what he calls "foreign language learning" (which, he says, is the characteristic method by which adults learn language in the formal classroom) from primary language acquisition by young children, and from secondary language acquisition by older children. He feels that primary and secondary acquisition can proceed in essentially similar ways, but he believes that the foreign language learning must inevitably proceed in a very different manner. He emphasizes different neuro-functional organizations that are available at different ages, however, and he appears to be blithely unconcerned with the differing social opportunities that strike me as so obvious. Until the differing effects of the social settings are better understood, I suggest that it is premature to grope about for more subtle neurological explanations.

which learners (either children or adults) must cope with massive onslaughts of the language. They struggle as best as they can to understand and to make their needs known, but receive little or no deliberate instruction in the form of lessons, assignments, vocabulary lists to memorize, or essays to compose. The classroom setting, of course, is the opposite: the situation in which students, of whatever age, are given deliberate instruction in their new language. They are asked to memorize words, phrases, paradigms, or dialogues, and they are led gradually through increasingly difficult levels of the language.*

Although many combinations and compromises between the two settings are possible, most foreign language learning (or acquisition) takes place under circumstances that can be easily assigned to one or the other. Children always acquire their first language in a purely naturalistic setting. High schools and colleges teach foreign languages in a purely classroom setting. Preadolescent children who go abroad with their families usually acquire their new language in a predominantly naturalistic setting. These children may encounter their new language in school, but they are typically subjected to relatively little deliberate instruction in the language. Foreign college students who

---

*The distinction I draw between naturalistic and classroom settings covers some of the same ground as the distinction that many students have drawn between language "acquisition" and language "learning" (e.g., Krashen, 1979). "Acquiring" includes the manner in which children absorb their first language, but it is presumed to be available to older learners as well. Acquiring takes place without conscious awareness of the rule system of the language and it does not require overt teaching. Learning, on the other hand, is based on the overt teaching of rules and their internalization by the student. Correction of errors is presumed to be useful for learning, but not for acquiring. Acquiring has typically taken place in naturalistic settings where the language is absorbed without systematic or self-conscious instruction. Learning grows out of lessons, planning, and deliberate effort, and it has often been fostered in the classroom. I want to focus more sharply on the external circumstances that evoke different learner (or acquirer) responses, and less specifically on the responses themselves, both because the external circumstances are more directly observable and because they are more subject to manipulation. For these reasons I prefer to draw my primary distinction between the two settings rather than between learning and acquiring. If we imagine that we can encourage students to rely less on learning and more on acquiring, we will have to help them by manipulating the settings and so we must begin by understanding the settings. In the end, however, I will argue that we can, in fact, use the classroom to encourage acquisition.

enroll in a course in English as a foreign language in this country are expected to exploit both settings. They face the classroom setting for a few hours each day, but everyone hopes they will also be able to profit from a more naturalistic contact with English speakers outside their formal classroom.

Most children before their teens acquire most of their language in a naturalistic setting; adolescents and adults are more often confined to the classroom. It has been argued that these contrasting settings are proper and appropriate to the contrasting talents of the different ages (e.g., Krashen, 1975), but children can be given classroom instruction, and adults do occasionally get into naturalistic settings, so age and setting are not logically, or inevitably, linked. I want to consider the differences between the settings with some care and to ask whether the more crucial advantages of the naturalistic setting might be mimicked in the classroom. If they could be mimicked, then the experience of child second language learners would have important implications for adults. What then are the differences between the two settings?

1. *Time.* First is the simple matter of time. Preadolescent children who are thrown into a school with a new language are likely to have few demands placed on them except for those that directly involve language. For several hours every day in school and, if they are able to see and play with their contemporaries, for several more hours after school, they will be exposed to the language. Perhaps they will even watch television in the evening. Most of their daily activities are not explicitly designed to teach the language, but they do so just as effectively as if they were. It is not unusual for children in a foreign situation to spend eight hours a day in an ideal environment for acquiring the language. It should cause no wonder if they learn at eight times the rate of high school students back home who have only one hour a day for their foreign language.

2. *Clean input.* In the classroom setting, where students are typically encouraged to talk by every possible means, they are also inevitably subjected to massive doses of imperfect or distorted speech. Even in those rare cases where the teacher has flawless control of the language, at least half of the language heard in the classroom usually comes from students, and this means that half of the language a student hears is less than perfect. To the extent

that natural processes of language acquisition still operate with students in a classroom, they have to operate on imperfect input. Incorrect patterns of pronunciation, syntax, and word usage are internalized and consolidated.

Imperfect input is a problem for students, whatever their age. Selinker, Swain, and Dumas (1975) describe the French spoken by children in a French immersion program in Toronto. These children came from English-speaking families, but they learned to use French easily in school, even when speaking among themselves. They had few contacts with children from French-speaking homes, however, and the result was that they had to model their French, in considerable part, on one another. Learning from those whose French was not native, their new language showed substantial influence of English. My own sixteen-year-old American daughter learned to speak a very modest amount of German at a French lycée, but, from her classmates, her German acquired a spectacular French accent. As a result of mutual adjustments to one another's distortions, students often emerge from foreign language training communicating rather well with each other, but then find it difficult to understand a native speaker (Postovsky, 1974). Students reinforce each other's bad habits.

A learner in a naturalistic setting, on the other hand, hears the language only as spoken by native speakers—clean data. Any contribution of unconscious acquisitional processes serves to provide the learner with nativelike abilities.

3. *Implicit instruction.* To those who have struggled with deliberate classroom instruction, the most astonishing thing about children is that they seem to be able to learn so successfully even without any deliberate instruction. With no careful (or even careless) explanations of how the language works, grade-school children still seem able to abstract from their environment whatever it is they need to know about their new language. They are able to model their speech on what they hear and to use it in an increasingly structured and accurate manner. This ought to make us wonder whether adults need as much explicit instruction as we usually offer them.

4. *Unselected and unsequenced data.* In the classroom we almost always take for granted the need for carefully selected and carefully graded materials. It is even hard to imagine how we

would design the lessons of a language course without worrying a great deal about order and sequence. Obviously, or so it would seem, the student cannot be expected to dive into the full language and immediately start to swim. He has to be guided, stroke by stroke.

And yet, preadolescent children do what we think adult learners cannot do. We casually put children into situations where they are barraged by the foreign language. We confidently, and correctly, expect them to emerge a few months later understanding what they hear and answering back. Perhaps sequencing is not so necessary as we assume. Would we be more successful if we threw adult learners more dramatically into the fray?

Before we too rashly abandon lesson sequencing, however, we ought to recognize that sequencing is not really absent even in the most naturalistic of settings. In talking with an imperfect speaker, adult or child, sensitive people always adjust their language to the perceived ability of the learner. A large amount of work has been done in recent years on "caretaker talk," the language used by adults and older children when speaking to small children. It seems abundantly clear that the adjustments made by parents and other caretakers facilitate the child's comprehension and make the language easier to learn (Ferguson, 1971; Slobin, 1975; Snow and Ferguson, 1977). The investigation of "caretaker talk" parallels closely studies of "foreigner talk," the language used when speaking to foreigners who control the language poorly (Ferguson, 1975; Wagner-Gough and Hatch, 1975; Freed, 1980). Like the talk used by caretakers, the talk used with foreigners is intended to make comprehension easier, and surely it does. We all have a subtle ability to fine tune our language to the perceived ability of our audience.

We have more inhibitions about simplifying for the sake of a foreigner than for the sake of a child, however, and foreign children probably benefit from the freedom we feel with children generally. It may seem condescending to simplify our language too much for an adult, but with a child we have no such qualms. We need to simplify, even for our own children, at least to the extent of avoiding overly learned or exotic vocabulary, and the extra simplification needed for a foreign child is unlikely to carry much stigma.

Both adults and other children who deal with a foreign child are usually quite willing and quite able to simplify their own language to whatever extent seems helpful. They avoid less common words; they pronounce with clarity; they repeat; they use one word at a time; they do anything at all to their speech if it helps to get their meaning across. As the child begins to learn, those around him naturally and gradually adjust their own speech upward. As a result, the foreign child, even in the most naturalistic setting imaginable, is exposed to a graded situation. The grading is achieved, however, only by the intuitive reactions of other speakers. The language is adjusted, on the spot, for the sake of the child. I suspect that this intuitive adjustment, always sensitive to the child's immediate needs, produces a more successful grading than even the most sophisticated textbook writer can ever achieve.

5. *Focus on meaning.* The absence of planned selection of materials implies still another characteristic of the naturalistic setting: the concern for meaning. Recent observations of first language learners have shown that parents consistently focus on meaning. Children's syntactic errors are rarely corrected and, except in indulgent amusement, they may not even be noticed. Confusions in meaning, on the other hand, are carefully attended to (Brown, Cazden, and Bellugi, 1969; Ervin-Tripp, 1971). Surely the same is true of child second language learners in naturalistic settings. What matters is not whether they get the gender or verb form right, but whether they get their coats on at recess time. Teachers, age mates, and everyone else who deals with a child immersed in a foreign setting must work hard to convey meaning. The child must constantly struggle to understand.

This consistent focus on meaning is in stark contrast to the energies expended in a typical classroom setting. Here, a terrible effort is focused on mere form. This is most woefully true of phonological and grammatical pattern drills, but, to a greater or lesser degree, almost every explicit pedagogical technique gives notably greater attention to structure than is provided in the naturalistic setting. Words, phrases, and sentences are regularly dealt with out of context. They never lack a context in a naturalistic setting (Oller, 1971).

6. *Emphasis on vocabulary.* The urgent importance of meaning inherent in naturalistic settings focuses attention on vocabulary. It is the vocabulary that carries the primary semantic load of

most messages, and that most ordinary speakers feel to be the salient part of their language. If they are really struggling to communicate, it is words more than anything else that learners need. If they can understand enough words they can hope to understand a message even if they have to rely on redundancy and context to fill in the details. If they can mouth a few words they can get out a message even if it has sloppy phonology, no morphology, and very little syntax.

Even the youngest second language learners realize that the vocabularies of their two languages differ. They are able to compare the vocabularies of their languages, and they realize the importance of selecting words from the proper language. The language used by beginning second language learners, like the earliest ventures of first language learners, usually consists of single words—"hello," "where?," "come," "hot"—or at least single formulas—"good morning," "thank you." Even accomplished speakers tend to reduce their language to single words or short sequences when attempting primitive communication with early learners. When the focus is on meaning, vocabulary becomes all important; pronunciation and syntax can be left, to a considerable extent, to shift for themselves.

In contrast to the naturalistic setting, learners in classroom settings typically devote a large proportion of their attention to embarrassing pronunciation and to mysteriously arbitrary grammar. Sometimes this is disguised in the form of dialogues to be memorized, or as patterns to be practiced. However, teachers always seem to feel an obligation to help their students master not only the words but, even more importantly, the patterns by which the words are expressed and combined.

7. *Lack of concern for errors.* The minimal explicit attention to grammar typical of the naturalistic setting means, in turn, that there is far less anguish about errors. With preadolescents, as with infants, we expect mistakes; but we routinely and calmly expect these mistakes gradually to take care of themselves. With a classroom of adults we always worry that uncorrected mistakes will lead to bad habits and that these will later be difficult to cure. With children we have such sublime confidence that the errors will be overcome that we ignore them so long as they do not interfere with the message that the child is trying to get across. We are pleased and delighted to be able to communicate at all. We

forget the errors that inevitably creep into the learner's speech. We may even cherish the errors of the ten-year-old second language learner almost as much as we cherish the baby talk of the two-year-old.

8. *Priority of comprehension.* Finally, the naturalistic and classroom settings differ in the relative importance of reception and production. Indeed, much of what has been covered in the first seven points can be summarized as the contrast between a focus on reception and a focus on production. Sequencing materials is more difficult and haphazard in reception than in production, for the learner cannot control what the other person will say. Meaning, in particular the meaning of words, is all important to one who would understand, while grammar is relatively unimportant and concern for errors is much reduced. I suggest that, except for the difference in time and the insistent importance of communication that is imposed by the brutal realities of the naturalistic setting, the most crucial difference between the naturalistic and the conventional classroom settings is the focus on comprehension. This is also the variable that is most susceptible to mimicry in the classroom.

Age and Ability

As languages are taught and learned today, there is a close correlation between age and setting. Prepubertal children generally acquire their skills in naturalistic settings while adolescents and adults are more likely to receive classroom instruction. It has been argued that these contrasting settings are proper and appropriate to the different ages, and that the ability of post-adolescents to profit from a naturalistic setting diminishes sharply at the very time that their ability to profit from the classroom setting rises (e.g., Krashen, 1975). The evidence for this is by no means unambiguous, however, and it suffers from our ignorance of what would really happen to an adult in an ideal naturalistic situation. It may also suffer from an exaggerated idea of the ease with which children learn. We cannot hope to understand the effects of age unless we distinguish carefully between the contrasting settings. In similar settings, then, how do the experiences of children and adults compare?

First, it is woefully clear that children do no better in a classroom setting than adults. The presumed aptitude of children for language learning has always provided the rationale for offering Foreign Language in Elementary Schools (FLES—everything needs an acronym), but anyone who keeps his eyes open while looking at the results of FLES programs will have to conclude that grade-school children have no advantage whatsoever over their older sisters and brothers. Indeed, the younger children do far worse. It is FLES's unhappy record that a stint of several years in elementary school foreign language study gives students only a very modest headstart when they reach high school. Often students who have endured years of FLES start right at the beginning again when they reach high school. They sit in the same classroom with those who have never studied the language at all. (See Oller and Nagato, 1974, for a judicious appraisal of the value of FLES programs.)

Supporters of FLES make the entirely erroneous assumption that, because children appear to learn language easily when transported to a foreign country and immersed in a foreign language, they will also learn easily when given instruction in an American classroom. All the evidence goes flat out against this fanciful belief, and it can only be held by someone who refuses to pay attention to the sharp distinction between classroom and naturalistic settings. Let us then be rid of any notion that our problems can be solved in the elementary schools. High school students clearly learn more rapidly than elementary school children when limited to formal instruction.

When we turn to a comparison between high school students and college students we must remember the rule of thumb that equates two years of a foreign language in high school with a single year in college. Once again the older students move faster. Graduate students, moreover, seem generally to be expected to move along somewhat more quickly than undergraduates. As long as we confine our comparisons to the classroom setting, it is clear that, at least until the twenties, age confers a consistent advantage.

When we turn to the naturalistic setting, the evidence is more complex, but hardly less decisive. First, it can hardly be disputed that children of all ages, when living in naturalistic settings, can learn a second language substantially more quickly than children learn their first language. Once again, age confers an advantage.

Second, the most careful studies all show that older preadolescent children learn more quickly than younger children. Ervin-Tripp tested English-speaking children who had been thrown into French language schools near Geneva, Switzerland; after some months, the eight- and nine-year-olds did substantially better on several measures of French ability than did the six- and seven-year-olds (Ervin-Tripp, 1974). Snow and Hoefnagel-Höhle obtained similar results in a study of English-speaking children who went to Dutch schools. On several measures of morphology, vocabulary, sentence repetition, and translation, speed of learning increased right through adolescence (Snow and Hoefnagel-Höhle, 1978). Thus, in the naturalistic setting, just as in the classroom setting, age confers a consistent advantage. At least until adolescence, the older the child, the more quickly is the foreign language learned.

The evidence in favor of age is complicated by two factors, however. First, it is more decisive for vocabulary and grammar than for pronunciation. The persistence of foreign accents among postadolescents and adults can hardly be dismissed, although some workers argue that under proper conditions even pronunciation problems can be overcome (Hill, 1970; Neufeld, 1979). Even in pronunciation, as Neufeld points out (1980), a distinction must be made between receptive and productive skills, and adults seem to be able to achieve nativelike receptive competence for phonology with no special difficulty, even when problems in production persist. In any case, the persistence of foreign accents should not blind us to the fact that, when they have adequate motivation and opportunity, many adolescents and adults do achieve nativelike fluency in other areas of language. Second, there is evidence that even though adults have a decisive advantage over children at the early stages of language acquisition (even in pronunciation; see Snow and Hoefnagel-Höhle, 1977), they may eventually be overtaken and passed by the slower starting children. (See Krashen et al., 1979, for a summary of evidence for age differences.) Still, it seems clear that on most measures of language skill, except possibly for the final refinements of pronunciation, age confers an advantage in the naturalistic setting just as it does in the classroom setting.

In the face of the advantages that age apparently confers, it may seem odd that young children have so often been looked upon as so successful, but if we judge children to do better than adults, it is partly because we judge them by different standards. A child who, at the age of five, speaks exactly like a five-year-old will be judged to have achieved linguistic perfection. Who could ask for more? An adult who, after five years, still speaks with a pronounced foreign accent and makes occasional grammatical mistakes will never be judged to speak perfectly, even if, by most objective measures, the adult has learned far more than the child. His vocabulary is likely to be much larger; he will be able to converse on an array of topics that we would never expect to hear from a child and, if he makes grammatical errors, it is in part because he attempts more. His sentences may have a length and complexity that are well beyond the reach of the five-year-old. Obviously, we judge the five-year-old by a lower standard than we judge the thirty-year-old, and it is hardly surprising that the five-year-old comes off looking better. Ten-year-olds speak more elaborately than five-year-olds, and we look for a correspondingly higher level of achievement from them. Nevertheless, a level that would be fully adequate for a ten-year-old would still be insufficient for his father.

The experiences of my daughters, who were ten and sixteen when we took them to France, were probably quite typical. The ten-year-old was abandoned to the tender care of a French schoolmistress and thirty classmates, and the sixteen-year-old (safely past puberty, let it be noted) to the less tolerant or tender care of a French lycée. At the end of the year the two girls seemed to have learned approximately the same amount of French, although the sixteen-year-old was probably not quite as close as her younger sister to catching up with her contemporaries, so the ten-year-old might have been judged as "better." Eight years later, when they returned to France, the former sixteen-year-old remembered substantially more French than the former ten-year-old, so the long-term advantage certainly lay with the older child. In many ways, our casual observations have led us to exaggerate the achievements of children, especially quite young children. When looked at more carefully, older children, and even adults, turn out to have substantial advantages of their own.

Adults and Naturalistic Learning

At least until puberty, older children learn language more rapidly than do young children, and in the classroom the advantage of age continues well beyond puberty. The achievements of adults in a naturalistic setting, however, are more difficult to assess. Not only do we judge adults by different standards from those we use to judge children, but adults who have a strong motivation to learn a language so regularly submit to formal instruction, that undiluted naturalistic learning is unusual for them.

Such studies as have been done, however, do little to encourage the view that adults can do as well as children. Hanania (1974), Hanania and Gradman (1977), Schumann (1978a), and Shapira (1978) all cite case studies that chart the halting progress of Arabic- and Spanish-speaking adults who had moved to the United States but who avoided classroom instruction. The three adults described in these case studies made discouragingly little progress during the months of observation. Errors persisted, new constructions were learned only slowly, and even after many months in the United States communication remained difficult. None came close to meeting the standards we routinely expect of children.

Before we draw any depressing conclusions from these case studies, however, we have to remind ourselves that mere residence in a foreign country does not automatically bring with it an encouraging or useful naturalistic setting. Anyone who has had even tangential contact with an American diplomatic or business community in a foreign capital realizes that those who live and work among their own countrymen can rely on their native language, and may have little need and less incentive to learn anything at all of a new language. An adult does not easily find the kind of settings that children, at least until adolescence, more readily achieve.

Hanania makes it clear that her subject's opportunities for using English were sharply limited. Shapira's Guatemalan subject seems to have had more contact with English speakers, but her motivation was distinctly low. Schumann says that his Costa Rican subject "stuck quite close to a small group of Spanish speaking friends," and he seems to have avoided situations where English would be needed (1978a:97). Until we have studies of adults who have the same needs and opportunities as children and who, like children, are thrown full-time into a foreign language environment and surrounded by encouraging and talkative monolingual contemporaries, it would be premature to conclude that adults cannot profit as substantially as children from naturalistic settings.

What the case studies of Hanania, Schumann, and Shapira clearly demonstrate is that adults find it possible to isolate themselves from the surrounding language and to satisfy their needs within their own expatriate community. If those who take classes learn more than those who do not bother, this tells us something about varying needs and motivations, and something about the difficulty adults have in finding naturalistic settings. However, it tells us very little about the contrasting advantages of the settings. In the absence of anything better, adults are forced to fall back upon the classroom.

When we compare learners in similar settings, most of the advantages that have been attributed to children turn out to be illusory. Our impression of adult limitations may also be distorted by the salience of productive phonology and by the special phonological difficulties that a good many adults admittedly have. These difficulties, however, may have no profound or neurological significance at all, but may be due merely to superficial muscular maturation. As Neufeld points out, "the disability [in productive phonology] may be less psycholinguistic than psychomotor in nature" (Neufeld, 1980:296). The decline in the ability to learn other aspects of language is far less clear. Many adults do manage to acquire a near-native proficiency with grammar. Since they could not possibly achieve these skills entirely by explicit instruction in a classroom setting, we can be confident that adults retain some ability to exploit unconscious acquisitional processes.

It is true that some adults reach a plateau and seem never to climb above it. They manage to communicate with some degree of adequacy, and meet their perceived needs, but not even long years of exposure and practice saves them from markedly foreign phonology, broken syntax, or even a restricted vocabulary. This is the situation that has been aptly termed "fossilization" (Selinker, 1972). But since many adults do master grammar and vocabulary, fossilization, at least in these areas, is by no means inevitable or universal. When we recognize all the ways in which age confers decisive advantages, it is tempting to wonder whether we should seek the explanation for fossilization, not in profound maturational changes, but in lack of motivation, in social discrimination and isolation, and in superficial judgments made on the basis of imperfect phonology. Possibly fossilization is also encouraged by premature pressure to produce the language before it is adequately understood.

For, let us remember, there is one notable aspect of language that appears not to fossilize: comprehension. Most studies of language acquisition have focused on productive abilities, but production is only half the communication process, and with adequate exposure adults routinely achieve a nativelike control over the receptive half of a foreign language. However creaky their production, they gain full comprehension. Our pedagogy and tests are so strongly biased in favor of production that the "mere" ability to understand may not even be noticed. John Schumann, for instance, has given us an excellent case study of an adult who lacked classroom instruction (1978a). Schumann offers a sophisticated analysis of his Costa Rican subject's ability (or inability) to produce certain core syntactic constructions, and the data suggest that he made almost no progress in English during the ten months of the study. I suspect that our productive and syntactic biases are so pervasive that most readers of this case study did not even stop to wonder whether the informant's vocabulary might have expanded during this time or whether his comprehension could have improved. Nevertheless, the ability to comprehend certainly demonstrates an important skill. If adults can gain full understanding, then it is simply wrong to imagine that the natural ability to acquire language fades out with puberty.

When adults and children are compared in similar settings, adults turn out to have more advantages and fewer disabilities than is often imagined. It is by no means clear that they require formal instruction to learn a language, though it may be true that they are rarely patient enough to take the time to learn as children learn. It is, moreover, abundantly clear that adults face special social impediments that make it very difficult for them to achieve the kind of naturalistic setting that children more often achieve. Naturalistic settings, at ages when they are easily accessible, produce far more dramatic results than are seen in a classroom. It seems that the best course to follow when we are forced into a classroom would be to try to mimic the naturalistic setting in ways that would be most useful for an adult.

The Priority of Comprehension

Those who acquire language in a naturalistic setting—infants, child second language learners, even an occasional adult—can, at any point in their learning, always understand far more than they can say. This observation seems so banal to anyone who has watched a child learn a language, or to anyone who has tried to learn a language through use, that one could hardly think it could be doubted. However, with the characteristic psychological mistrust of the obvious, it has indeed been doubted (Bloom, 1974; Chapman, 1974; Clark, Hutcheson, and VanBuren, 1974; Clark, 1974; Ingram, 1974).

It is, to be sure, easy to exaggerate someone's understanding. If you say to a child, "Would you be able to bring me my slippers from under the table?" while looking at the slippers and pointing to them, a cooperative child need not understand much language in order to carry out the task. Getting the slippers does not demonstrate the child's high ability in English. Occasionally, moreover, children will use words or even fairly complex syntactical patterns at times and in situations where it is by no means certain that they have any clear understanding of their meaning. Sometimes it seems as if children simply generate patterns for the sheer pleasure of the generation, even if this means that they use them in inappropriate situations. This looks as though the children's productive ability may actually outstrip their ability to understand.

This claim, however, confuses two aspects of language. "Production," in this case, can only mean "production of form," such as the use of a word, the correct word order, or some detail of grammar. By "comprehension," on the other hand, we surely mean "comprehension of meaning." It is true that children occasionally learn to use a form without learning its meaning. We know this when they use a form—a word or a grammatically correct construction—in a semantically anomalous situation. To learn the form before its meaning, however, is not at all equivalent to learning to speak before learning to understand. We confuse the production/comprehension distinction with the form/meaning distinction because we so habitually link form to production and meaning to reception. From this biased outlook, it is easy to draw the erroneous conclusion that, since mastery of the form occasionally comes before mastery of meaning, then production must also occasionally come before reception.

In fact, however, before children can use a correct form, they must certainly have a sense of its "sounding right" in the speech of others. That is, they must have a receptive appreciation of its form before they can use it in a formally correct way. In parallel fashion, before they can use a form in its correct meaning, they must surely understand its meaning when used by others. From this point of view, production (of either form of meaning) always follows reception.

In the overwhelming majority of cases children have a sense of both meaning and form before they try to use them, and in some cases comprehension runs far ahead of production. There are reports of striking pathological cases that show that comprehension can far outstrip production (Curtiss, 1977; Lenneberg, 1962; MacNeilage, Rootes, and Allen, 1967), but there is also ample evidence that comprehension runs well ahead of production in normal children as well (Myklebust, 1957; Wolski, 1962; Ervin-Tripp, 1974). All observant parents notice that there is a time in their children's development when they can, when asked, point to their nose, eyes, or mouth, although they are still unwilling to use the words productively. Adults, too, typically learn to understand more than they can say. Nida (1971) describes a perfectly normal North American lawyer who had business in South America, and who read and understood Spanish perfectly but would not try to speak it.

All normal adults understand far more of their native language than they can produce. All of us understand vocabulary that we avoid using ourselves—technical terms, erudite words, the slang of a group not our own. All of us can easily understand many dialects that we cannot use actively. We even understand a few syntactical forms that we do not use, such as nonstandard forms in the case of standard speakers and vice versa, and we can untangle larger and more complex sentences than we habitually produce. This is a general characteristic of all mature speakers, and of course it is also true of children.

There are also ethnographic reports of societies in which adults are expected to learn language primarily through listening and understanding, and to postpone active production until after the language is learned. Sorenson (1967) writes about the Vaupés River area that straddles the Brazilian-Colombian border in the northwest Amazon. In this area men take wives from a different language group from their own. As a result, each longhouse group includes a core of men who share a first language along with their inmarrying wives who bring in a number of other languages. Children, therefore, are exposed to several languages in their home community, but their primary language is always their father's. Adults cultivate multilingualism, but they do not ordinarily try to speak a language before they know it. The idea of waiting to speak a language until one knows it is peculiar from our traditional view of language learning, but in the Vaupés River area the people feel that the reasonable way to learn is simply to listen until the language can be understood easily. Once that is accomplished, speaking is expected to follow with little difficulty. The method is dramatically successful; most adults in the area speak three, four, or more languages.

Navajo children are said to learn their language in a somewhat similar way. Navajo adults offer less encouragement to their children to speak than do Anglo-American adults. They even tend to feel that no one should attempt to use a skill–not even a language—until they know how to do it, and young Navajo are said to be rather silent by Anglo standards. At about the age of five or six they begin to talk more consistently, but by then they are able to follow reasonably correct standards (Gary Witherspoon, personal communication). Australian aborigines sometimes say "I can hear him but I cannot talk to him" to indicate their receptive, as opposed to productive, control of a language (Aram A. Yengoyan, personal communication).

Comprehension, of course, is far more difficult to study than production. We can listen to and transcribe what learners say and we can readily follow their progress in speaking through weeks and months of learning, but it is always difficult to be certain how much someone has understood. As a result, we have had relatively few studies of comprehension, but this is hardly an adequate excuse for the widespread but false assumption that learning a language is essentially equivalent to learning to speak. Once we grasp the evident truth that learners in naturalistic settings are always much more skillful at understanding than at speaking, we must also face the likelihood that the most fundamental stages of naturalistic language learning take place as the child learns to understand, and that most words and constructions are used actively only after they have become thoroughly familiar to the ear. Most studies of child language report only the final steps by which knowledge that has been acquired over a long period is at last activated in production.

I think we should take seriously the anecdotes we have all heard about occasional first language learners, and about some children immersed in a foreign language setting, who say almost nothing for many months after language is expected to begin. Finally, after everyone despairs, the child begins to talk, and when she finally does so, language comes with explosive rapidity. In such cases we can hardly imagine that learning begins only with the onset of the active use of the language. Learning has certainly been going on, quietly and invisibly, throughout the entire period of exposure. Progressively, steadily, a knowledge of the language is built up. Finally, once a critical threshold is crossed, the learner is ready for active use, but by then she is able to draw on a great fund of experience.

In naturalistic settings, comprehension always precedes production, but in our classrooms we manage to produce anomalous students who can produce sentences they cannot understand. A few of them learn to laboriously build up long and complex sentences that hew reasonably closely to native standards of syntax and morphology and that have understandable phonology, but when presented with the identical sentence at an unexpected moment they may find their minds are blank. This is a pathology of language that results from the pathologies of our classrooms.

Interference Errors and Natural Sequence Errors

The last few years have seen the growth of a bulky literature dealing with the source of errors made by second language learners. It was once taken for granted that interference from the native language explained most errors, and no mystery surrounds the interference that new learners display. When asked to speak early in their training, learners must cope simultaneously with a whole range of problems. They must push their jaw and tongue into unfamiliar positions, they must twist their vocal cords to produce unfamiliar intonations, they must get their words out in unfamiliar order, they must attach suffixes in unfamiliar places, and they should try, while doing all these things, to remember what those strange bits of noise are supposed to mean, and how they can add together to give a general meaning to what they are trying to say. Of course, there is no conceivable way in which they can do all these things simultaneously until they have acquired an extensive knowledge of every level of the language. Since early learners cannot possibly have this extensive knowledge, they are simply forced to fall back on their only relevant skill: their knowledge of their own native language. The result is massive interference (Newmark, 1966; Krashen, 1977).

It is so easy to point to examples of obvious phonological, syntactical, and even lexical interference, that it seems rash to question its importance. Nevertheless, there are problems with too easy an acceptance of interference. Wardhaugh (1974) has pointed to some theoretical difficulties with the principle, but the more interesting challenges come from observations of child second language learners who acquire their new language in naturalistic settings. A few studies (notably that of Dulay and Burt, 1974, but see also several of the papers in Hatch, 1978) have claimed that whatever their native language background, children who learn a second language go through essentially the same learning sequence, and this is even said to resemble the sequence through which infants move when learning their first language. The claim is thus made that many of the errors made by child second language learners should not be attributed to interference but to a natural learning sequence through which all children must move as they gradually approach mature standards.

There is also a gradually accumulating body of evidence that adults also tend to pass through a natural sequence, and the adult sequence also appears to be similar to that followed by children. Many adult errors can be attributed to overgeneralization of patterns in their new language rather than to interference from an earlier language (Corder, 1967; Bailey, Madden, and Krashen, 1974; Richards, 1973). Classroom instruction is in danger of distorting this natural sequence in two ways. First, the syllabus followed in a classroom is unlikely to reflect the natural sequence, and second the attempt to suppress errors makes it difficult to exploit the sequence. It is hardly surprising that large numbers of interference errors are the result.

To claim that even children who acquire a second language in a naturalistic setting show *no* interference from their first language would surely go too far, however. Every careful diary study of child second language learners shows unambiguous evidence of interference. Leopold, the most careful diarist of all, gives examples of clear syntactic interference between English and German in his young daughter's speech (Leopold, 1954). Snow and Hoefnagel-Höhle (1977) say that even the youngest English-speaking learners of Dutch had unmistakable accents. At the same time it seems clear that interference is a far more serious and persistent problem for adult learners who pursue their studies in a classroom than for children whose second language is acquired without explicit instruction. The difficult question, of course, is whether it is the setting or the age of the learner that is primarily responsible for the difference.

If age is the explanation, then we may simply have to resign ourselves to interference when adults learn a foreign language, but to the degree that it is the setting that makes the difference we would have some hope of minimizing the effect of interference if we could manipulate the setting.

Sorting out the effects of age and setting will be difficult until we have more thorough studies of adults who learn a new language in naturalistic circumstances and of young children who learn in the classroom. Only then will we be able to examine age and setting as independent variables. While acknowledging that the final evidence is not yet available, the cautious view would now seem to be that problems of interference, at least in phonology, and possibly in grammar, increase with age, but that some of the interference problems that adults so often face are attributable to the setting in which they have characteristically had to learn the language. We are challenged to manipulate whatever aspects of the setting would minimize interference.

Conclusions

Perhaps it is too much to expect most adults to master a new phonology, and perhaps we should not care. Many adults may stop refining their grammar before they have achieved a native level of perfection, but there is no reason at all to imagine that adults are in any way limited in their ability to acquire vocabulary, nor are adults handicapped in learning to understand. Enough adults also master the grammar of a new language to keep us from becoming fatalistic or from setting our standards too low. Adults can learn languages and, under proper conditions, rather better in most respects than children. We should begin to help them, instead of letting our deficient pedagogy get in their way.

For we must remember that, beyond any possible advantages of a hypothetical "critical period," children have one other advantage so overwhelming that one wonders why other factors need to be sought: children far more easily and readily find the kind of naturalistic setting that is most useful in fostering language. The older a child grows, the more difficult the naturalistic setting is to achieve, and the real difficulties begin about college age. College professors are less tolerant than third-grade teachers when students do not know the language of the classroom, and once the years of education are over, and especially as one becomes established in one's own family with its own well-established language, it becomes increasingly difficult to escape one's own language or to find the naturalistic settings in which a new language is most readily learned. The forty-year-old adult can hardly imagine subjecting himself to life with a strange family in a strange land in order to learn a language. Nor would the family welcome the balding forty-year-old with the same enthusiasm with which it welcomes the seventeen-year-old *au pair* girl.

Reasonable pedagogy for adults ought to struggle against the limitations imposed by the social setting. Hanania (1974) studied an Arabic speaker whose progress in English was halting but who did make notable progress during some months when she cared regularly for a neighbor's small children. Then she had no choice but to use English, and for the first time she could do so without embarrassment. It should not be taken as a joke to suggest that English would be more effectively taught by using new foreign students to staff the nation's day-care centers than by herding them into TEFL classes. There are studies that seem to show that foreign university students who are tossed into classes in their own specialized areas of interest learn English just as quickly as those who are forced to take courses in English as a foreign language (Upshur, 1968; Mason, 1971). These studies ought to cause far more anguish and self-doubt among TEFL teachers than they have. The real challenge for TEFL teachers in this country should not be so much what to do in their classrooms, as how to get their students out of their classrooms and into naturalistic settings.

Nevertheless, formal foreign language instruction will continue, so we are challenged to look for ways of overcoming the inherent disadvantages of the classroom and to imitate, as best as possible, the advantages of the naturalistic setting. When we review the list of factors that distinguish the naturalistic setting from classroom instruction, the areas most susceptible to manipulation are all related to comprehension.

We cannot expect to do much about the total time available for studying a foreign language, and it is difficult to imagine a classroom without explicit instruction or without some sort of explicit selection and even sequencing of materials. We can, however, certainly make a choice about the balance of emphasis that we want to give to comprehension and production, and if we shift toward a greater emphasis on comprehension, that could imply many other changes that would bring some approximation to naturalistic learning. With modern tapes and records, a focus on comprehension would allow early learners to hear the language only as spoken by native speakers and never to be corrupted by the errors of their classmates. When working for understanding, the eccentricities of grammatical structure become relatively unimportant. People can learn to understand a great deal without a full grasp of the morphological or even syntactical details of the language. To understand, they need to build their receptive vocabulary as quickly as possible, but details of grammar, particularly the fussy irregularities that are such a burden to other early language learners, can be postponed. Irregularities such as genders, or irregular verbs, are far easier to recognize than to reproduce. These grammatical details can be left for later. Errors are far less evident in a student who is trying only to understand and the inevitability of error becomes less of a threat.

Of course, the time will come when students will want to speak, but before they are pushed to do so they should have built up an extensive knowledge of the language on which to draw. When they begin to speak they will, of course, still make mistakes, but everything we know about language acquisition in naturalistic settings suggests that errors should not be too strenuously corrected. Many should be regarded as developmental errors that will take care of themselves as the learner gains more practice with understanding the language, as he becomes sensitive to its sounds and organization, and as he grows more skillful at monitoring his own speech.

As long as a student is studying a language away from a community where it is spoken, however, there will be insurmountable difficulties in gaining adequate practice with speaking. If students practice with each other, as they do in most foreign language classrooms, they will surely corrupt each other. In the absence of willing native speakers there is no way to get entirely adequate practice in speaking. Perhaps the main effort at speaking should be left until the student finally goes traveling.

If, however, learners are to gain a fluent command over their new language, a time must come when they launch forth on their own and engage in real conversations. It has been the pitiful experience of many students who have been relatively successful in conventional foreign language classrooms to find, when trying their wings in real life, that they can use convincing enough phonology and syntax to evoke a beautiful but quite totally mysterious symphony of prose in response. In such cases, the interlocutor judges the capacity of the learner by what she hears. Hearing some reasonably adequate language, she reponds in kind or, more likely, at a somewhat more advanced level, since fluent speakers tend to talk at a level that is just a bit ahead of the perceived ability of the learner—child or adult. When a learner's productive ability is too close to his receptive ability, he talks with unwarranted confidence. Not being able to understand the responses, he cannot participate in a conversation. In spite of his productive dexterity, the conversation ends. Aborted conversations provide little chance for practice, and the result is frustration, discouragement, and the impression that the language never seems to reach a usable level.

When receptive ability is decisively ahead of productive ability, as it always is in naturalistic learning, the new learner will give more accurate and more useful signals. He may speak imperfectly, he may even massacre the language, but to that very degree he will signal to his interlocutor that he cannot cope with language that goes beyond a certain level. The interlocutor will then be more likely to adjust her speech level downward, and if she adjusts it to the point where she can be understood, the learner will have the rewarding experience of successful communication. However disorganized his own speech, he is more likely than his more fluent classmate to come away from the encounter satisfied at having participated in a two-way conversation. Having solicited language at a level he can understand, moreover, the less skillful speaker will have a chance to profit from the encounter. Thus, too much skill at talking can actually be a deterrent to learning. It sends wrong signals and so dulls the effectiveness of natural conversations. Perhaps we should encourage all learners to make enough blunders to evoke the level of language with which they can cope. That is one function of broken speech. We undermine that function when we insist on too much accuracy in the early stages of language learning. Paradoxically, the best way to equip a student to take full advantage of natural conversations and to use them to acquire a productive capacity, is probably to minimize attention to production.

It is important to remember that not all of the advantages lie with the children. The ability to learn a language improves steadily through childhood and it cannot collapse entirely at puberty. Adults surely maintain many of the cognitive advantages that older children have over their younger sisters and brothers, but in most conventional language pedagogy we burden adults with terrible demands for early production that we never ask of small children. These demands cause nothing but discouragement and delay.

If an emphasis on comprehension offers such promise, why has production been so strenuously encouraged? We can blame the mistaken notion that language requires a kind of behavior—physical movement—and that behavior requires practice and drill. The more quickly and thoroughly we shake ourselves free from our behaviorist assumptions, the more quickly will we be able to help our students gain the knowledge of new languages that they need.

Teachers have only limited room for maneuver. They can try to help their students find naturalistic settings outside their classroom, but only in class do they really have control. The most effective means for bringing some of the advantages of the naturalistic setting into the classroom appears to be to focus on comprehension and to devise every conceivable way to encourage students to understand the new language as rapidly as possible. In the following chapters I turn to some specific techniques that can help reach this goal.

Reading a Mixed Language

Once we free ourselves from the traditional view of foreign language instruction—that we must teach people to speak— unorthodox but effective ways of helping students suddenly become plausible. In this chapter and the next I discuss two unconventional experiments in language instruction that I helped to develop and try out at the University of Michigan. One is a method for teaching reading, and the other is directed toward aural comprehension. Neither method is fully developed and ready, in all its details, to be widely applied, but the experiments I describe here are intended to offer suggestions and to stimulate ideas about the wide range of methods that become possible as soon as we abandon the effort to teach production in early language instruction. The methods could be modified in many ways. They might be combined with each other, and they will have to be combined with many other techniques in order to develop an integrated comprehension approach.

In recent decades most introductory language courses have begun with a vigorous effort directed at the spoken language. Many people who would like to be able to read, however, have little hope or expectation of using a language in conversation. People really do sometimes learn to read languages, for pleasure and profit, even when their aural and oral skills are minimal. Even in the monolingual United States, graduate students are still occasionally required to demonstrate their ability to read foreign languages, and the reading courses offered to these graduate students do not deserve to be stigmatized as vulgarly practical and then shuffled off on a low-status member of the department. Those who would like to avoid the agonies posed by the spoken language deserve to be taken seriously, and there is no reason to give such people training in the spoken language unless that proves to be the most efficient route toward reading. We should be willing to experiment with techniques that lack any aural component at all.

The technique I describe in this chapter omits work with the spoken language, but it also incorporates another, and far more radical, proposal: I suggest that we offer students texts that are intimate mixtures of their native and their new languages. I will describe texts that start with only modest deviations from the students' native language, but that then, as the pages and chapters pass by, shift progressively in the direction of the target language. In this way, the forms of the new language are gradually introduced into a linguistic system that the student already knows well and, at every stage, the language used will be sufficiently full and complex to express ideas that are of interest to adults.*

Texts in a mixed language have several attractive features. By capitalizing on the ability of students to mix their languages, we exploit the tendency of the linguistic context to narrow the range of possible meanings that new words and constructions could have. By retaining enough that is familiar, we let students practice, at every stage, with fully adult texts.No one need ever be reduced to the insulting level of Dick and Jane that is the unhappy lot of most beginning language students. Whatever materials students find interesting can be adapted to the method. With materials of high intrinsic interest, students can be motivated to continue to read, not only from a long-term desire to learn the language, but also from a more immediate eagerness to find out how the plot develops.

The method also allows a radical reordering of the sequence of topics presented to the students. In particular, it becomes

---

*Mixed language texts are by no means as radical as they may appear to some readers. Indeed, they are simply a variant of the technique of interlinear translations and interlinear glosses that goes back to the Middle Ages (Kelly, 1969:142–49). More recently, Halmuth H. Schaefer (1963) devised a scheme for teaching German that is very similar to the program in French that I describe in this chapter, and R.K. Tongue (n.d.) has used the method for teaching Indonesian. Nevertheless, the method hardly occupies the mainstream of twentieth century language instruction, and it will surely strike a good many language teachers as bordering on the bizarre. Its advantages deserve to be considered before too hasty rejection, however.

possible to present grammatical materials more systematically and more usefully than in most language courses. In the next section I give some examples of the steps I have offered in a program for French reading, and it will be seen that the method allows the most general and pervasive features of the language to be presented first, while its more irregular and idiosyncratic aspects are postponed until later. In a more conventional course, when the students are expected to start speaking from the first day, the very first lesson must touch upon everything. It must include something about pronunciation; it must introduce words of several grammatical categories; it must at least hint at a few rules of grammar so that the words can be joined together into meaningful phrases and sentences. When so many topics must be touched upon, no one of them can be dealt with in any depth. Each topic of grammar (pronouns, tenses, the gender system, etc.) comes typically to be spread across many lessons, and students have trouble gaining any overall perspective of the linguistic processes involved.

By using mixed texts it becomes possible to describe a linguistic process briefly and then introduce the major features of this process into the text, but to ignore the irregularities and details, leaving them to be absorbed gradually through long exposure. In French, for instance, gender and number work together in an interrelated system that is expressed through articles, adjectives, and nouns. The general characteristics of the system can be explained in a few short paragraphs. This is enough to allow learners to recognize the forms, though not enough to let them reproduce them accurately. The French forms of the articles and of the adjective suffixes can then be introduced into a practice text. If the context into which these new forms are introduced is entirely familiar, learners can easily get a feeling for what is new, even while most of their attention is directed to understanding the context of what they are reading. The overall principles of the system can be learned quite easily in this way, while its irregularities (such as the irregular feminine and plural forms of many French adjectives) will be learned more slowly. When active and accurate production is required, these irregularities require a lengthy and detailed description and a long struggle to learn, but if the principles of the system are clear, and if active production is not needed, the irregularities gradually fall into place without so much difficulty. Other aspects of the language can be introduced in the same way.

A French Reading Program

I have developed, and tried with students, a series of lessons designed to help them read French (Burling, 1978a). Each lesson consists of two parts: first, a few pages that summarize one or more features of the French language in a way that should help the learner get through a written text; and second, a reading passage that incorporates those features.

The following paragraphs describe some of the steps through which I have led students and they will give a concrete idea of the method. Short passages adapted from "La dernière classe" by Alphonse Daudet illustrate these levels. Students who actually use the materials, of course, practice with much longer passages.

    1. *Word order.* The first and most pervasive aspect of French to which students must grow accustomed is word order. Where French word order is like English nothing at all needs to be said, and a few paragraphs are enough to help the student recognize and understand the major ways in which French word order differs from English: (1) object pronouns precede verbs; (2) adjectives often follow nouns; (3) negatives usually come in two parts that surround the verb; (4) subjects and verbs are more regularly exchanged to form questions than in English. It is also helpful at this early stage to point out that the definite article is sometimes used in French where it would not appear in English. Many other details of French word order and word use can be passed over in silence. Even where the order differs slightly from English, the meaning will usually emerge quite easily and students will soon become accustomed to the French pattern through the examples in their reading. Here is the first of many areas where a comprehension approach allows a much simpler treatment than a production approach. Students who must talk need detailed guidance on many aspects of word order. Most of word order can be left implicit for those who need only to understand.

The only French words I use at this stage are the most common words for negation—*ne ... pas.* English equivalents for these could be found, but they would be so artificial that the simpler solution seems to be to introduce this single French form from the very beginning. I use French punctuation from the start.

With this introduction as a background, students have no trouble with passages such as this closely literal, word for word, translation from French into English.

That morning–there I was very late for to go to the school, and I had great fear of to be scolded, all the more that Mr. Hamel us had told that he us would question on the participles, and I *ne* of them knew *pas* the first word. A moment the idea to me came to miss the class and to take my course across fields.

The weather was so warm, so clear!

One heard the blackbirds to whistle at the edge of the forest, and in the meadow of Rippert, behind the sawmill, the Prussians who did the exercise. All that me tempted much more than the rule of the participles; but I had the strength of to resist, and I ran very quickly toward the school.

2. *Gender and number.* As noted earlier, gender and number unite into a single system in French. This system embraces the articles, which include several of the most common words of the French language, along with plural suffixes of nouns and the feminine and plural suffixes of adjectives. The system is not terribly complex, but it is so pervasive that it provides a strategic point of entry into the language. It is convenient, at the same time, to introduce the very common prepositions *de* and *à* which frequently form contractions with the articles, and also the closely related pronouns *y* and *en*.

When this set of common words is introduced into reading passages that otherwise continue to be formed from English words, the students can quickly get a sense of one important component of French grammar.

In passing in-front-of *la* town-hall, I saw that there was *du* crowd stopped near *du* little screen *aux* posters. Since two years, it is *de* there that to-us are come all *les* bad-*es* news, *les* battles lost, *les* requisitions, *les* orders *de la* headquarters; and I thought without myself to stop:

«What is-it that there is again?»

Then, as I crossed *la* square in running, *le* blacksmith Wachter, who was there with his apprentices in process *de* to-read *la* poster, to me cried:

«*Ne* yourself hurry *pas* so much, little one; you *y* will-arrive anyway enough soon *à* your school!»

I believed that he himself teased *de* me, and I entered all breathless in *la* little-*e* courtyard *de* Mr. Hamel.

Ordinarily, *au* commencement *de la* class, there was *un* great uproar that one heard as-far-as in *la* street, *les* desks opened, closed, *les* lessons that one repeated very loud all together *en* oneself plugging *les* ears for better to-learn, and *la* great ruler *du* teacher that tapped on *les* tables:

«*Un* bit *de* silence!»

Following the gender-number system, I devote a lesson to the four words *qui, que, où,* and *quand.* These are difficult words, for each is used in a number of distinct ways, and since they differ markedly from familiar English usage, they need special treatment. A reading passage that incorporates these words in their varied uses allows sentences to approach the original French considerably more closely.

Next, a score of very common French words are introduced. These include such conjunctions, adverbs, adjectives, and prepositions as *et, mais, comme, très, autre, beaucoup, avec,* and *dans,* and three nouns: *jour, père,* and *chose.* These words are relatively straight equivalents of English words, and this makes them quite easy to learn; but since all of them appear constantly in the text, turning them into French allows the passage to assume a considerably more French appearance. This gives the students a satisfying sense of progress. Following this, the students are ready for something more complex.

3.   *Pronouns.* The French system of personal pronouns is considerably more complex than the English system, but all the pronouns can be introduced together and explained as a system. A single chart can display all the pronouns in a clear order and in a form the student can easily consult. Certain specific problems need special discussion. The use of *on* and the difference between *tu* and *vous* need to be discussed briefly, and a somewhat fuller explanation is needed for the distinction between direct and indirect object pronouns and for the reflexives. Learning the pronouns is made easier by the experience that the students have already had before they reach this lesson, for they will have grown accustomed to French word order and they will no longer be surprised to find object pronouns before the verb. Even the reflexive pronouns have appeared (translated as "myself," "yourself," etc.) and this eases the transition to the French forms. The section on pronouns does introduce more new words and more new grammatical materials than any of the earlier sections, however, and the reading passage must be correspondingly longer.

> *Je* counted *sur tout* this confusion *pour* to-reach *mon* bench *sans* to-be seen; *mais* just that *jour*-there *tout* was tranquil, *comme un* morning *de* Sunday. *Par la* window open-*e, je* saw *mes* classmates already distributed *à leurs* place-*s, et* Mr. Hamel, *qui* passed *et* repassed *avec la* terrible ruler *en* iron under *le* arm. It [was] necessary to-open *la* door *et* to-enter *au* middle *de* that great stillness. *Vous* imagine, if *je* was red *et* if *je* had fear!

4.   *Borrowing.* The burden of learning French is greatly eased for an English speaker because of the vast number of words we

have borrowed from French. Much of this vocabulary is transparent to an English speaker, but certain aspects of the borrowing can be explained in a way that will help the learner recognize borrowings and interpret them correctly. Words that are sufficiently similar in the two languages can then be included in their French form in the reading passages and this immediately and easily converts a substantial proportion of the passages to French.

> *Eh* well, no. Mr. Hamel *me regard*-ed *sans* anger *et me* said *très* softly: «Go quickly *à ta place, mon* little Frantz; *nous* [were] going to-*commence sans toi.*»
>
> *Je* leaped-over *le* bench *et je me* sat quickly *à mon* desk. Then only, *un* bit relieved *de ma* fright, *je* noticed *que notre* teacher had *sa* handsome-*e* frock-coat green-*e, son* ruffled-shirt pleated finely *et la* skull-cap *de* silk black-*e* embroider-*ée qu'il ne* wore *que les jours d'inspection ou de distribution de* prizes.

5. *Verbs and tenses.* As every schoolchild knows, the most difficult aspect of French grammar is the verb system, and it poses by far the most difficult problems for the lesson designer. It is the only aspect of French grammar that I felt had to be spread out across a number of lessons, for it is simply too complex to introduce all at once. My materials introduce some of the most common verb suffixes quite early, including infinitive and participial suffixes, and the suffixes of two common tenses: the past definite and the present. Later I introduce the remaining simple tenses, and still later the compound tenses together with the auxiliary verbs that form them. As with adjective endings, I begin by simply attaching the French verb suffixes to the English words, except in those cases where the French verb is enough like English to be used in its French form.

To start with, only the first conjugation endings are used. This limitation conforms to the principle that the first priority is to provide a feeling for the overall system of the language. Once the system is well understood, the student will be able to tackle the numerous irregularities with less difficulty. To simplify the student's task, even irregular verbs are translated as if they are regular. The French verb *faire* 'do,' for instance, is highly irregular, but it appears in the passages in such guises as do-*é*. This could stand in place of an original *fait* (the original past participle of *faire*) but the learner need never be concerned with whether the do-*é* that he encounters actually stands for the verb *faire* or for some other verb that is regular and that has a similar meaning.

Suffixes of the second and third conjugations and of irregular verbs are left until last. It seems best to give the students a chance to grow accustomed to the regular suffixes before burdening them with all the irregular forms. Eventually, of course, the irregularities must be faced, but it is far easier to recognize them than to produce them, and it is easier to recognize them after the regular forms are understood.

The passage that follows shows several stages that include progressively more details of the verb. Part way through this sequence it seems that some sort of threshold has been crossed so that the passage has become more French than English. At that point, I stop italicizing the slowly accumulating French and begin, instead, to italicize the gradually disappearing English.

> Besides, *toute la classe* had some *chose d'extraordinaire et de* solemn. *Mais ce qui me* surprise-*a le plus, ce* was *de* see-*er au* back *de la* room, *sur les* benches *qui* stay-*aient* empty-*s* ordinarily, *des* people *du* village seat-*és et* silent *comme nous, le* old *Hauser avec son* three-cornered-hat, *le* former mayor, *le* former postman, *et* then *d'autres personnes* still. *Tout ce* people-*là* appear-*ait* sad-*e; et* Hauser had bring-*é un* old primer eat-*é aux* edges *qu'il* hold-*ait* wide open-*é sur ses* knees, *avec ses* big-*es* spectacles rest-*ées* across *des pages.*
>
> *While que je m'étonnais de tout cela,* M. *Hamel était* climb-*é dans sa chaire, et de la même voice* soft-*e et* serious-*e with-which il m'avait* receive-*é, il nous* say-*a:*
>
> «Mes *children, c'est la* last-*e* time *que je vous* do-*e la classe. L'order est* come-*é de Berlin de ne plus* teach-*er que l'allemend dans les* schools *de l'Alsace et de la Lorraine . . . Le* new teacher arrive tomorrow. Today *c'est votre* last-*e lecon de francais. Je vous* ask-*e d'être* very *attentifs.*
>
> Ces quelques *words me* overwhelm-*èrent.* Ah! *les misérables, voilà ce qu'ils avaient* post-*é à la* townhall.
>
> Ma *last-*e leçon de francais! . . .*
>
> *Et moi qui savais à* scarcely write-*er! Je ne* learn-*erais* therefore *jamais! Il faudrait* therefore *en* stay-*er là! . . . Comme je m'en* resent-*ais* now *du* time *lose-*é, des classes* miss-*ées à* chase-*ir les* bird's-nests *ou à faire des* sliding *sur la Saar! Mes* books *que* just now still *je trouvais si* tiresome-*s, si* heavy-*s à* carry-*er, ma grammaire, mon histoire* sacred-*e me* seem-*aient à present de* old-*s amis qui me feraient beaucoup de* pain *à quitter. C'est comme M. Hamel. L'idée qu'il allait partir, que je ne le verrais plus, me faisait* forget-*er les* punishments, *les* blows *de* ruler.
>
> Poor *homme!*

As one works from the most pervasive patterns of the language toward its more idiosyncratic and irregular features, one reaches forms that occur less and less frequently and that require correspondingly long passages to give the learner adequate practice. I offer students sections on negatives, interrogatives, relative pronouns, adverbs and adjectives, numbers, and prepositions. Individually, none of these cause any serious problem, but there is so much to be learned, so many details to be absorbed, that long passages are needed for practice. As the details accumulate, the reading passages approach ever more closely to French until only the least common items of vocabulary continue to be translated into English.

> C'est en l'honneur de cette dernière classe qu'il avait mis ses beaux *clothes* du *Sunday*, et maintenant je comprenais pourquoi ces vieux du village étaient venus s'asseoir au *end* de la *room*. Cela semblait dire qu'ils regrettaient de ne pas y être venus plus souvent, à cette *school*. C'était aussi comme une façon de *thank*-er notre *teacher* de ses quarante *years* de bon service, et de *pay*-er leurs *respects* à la *nation* qui s'en *disappear*-ait . . .
>
> J'en étais là de mes réflexions, quand j'entendis appeler mon nom. C'était mon tour de réciter. Que n'aurais-je pas donné pour pouvoir dire tout au *full* cette fameuse *rule* des *participles*, bien *loud*, bien clair, sans une faute; mais je me *blunder*-ai aux premiers *words*, et je restai *up à me sway*-er dans mon *bench*, le coeur gros, sans *dare*-er *raise*-er la tête.

6. *Building vocabulary.* The final lesson consists of some suggestions about how to go about building vocabulary. The conventions of French dictionaries are described, but students are encouraged to read widely and to use a dictionary as little as possible. They are urged to try, as much as possible, to absorb the meaning of words gradually as they are faced in context instead of attempting to commit too many to memory by brute force.

The reading passage for this final lesson is given in its full original French. The student is encouraged to look up as few words as possible and to try, instead, to gain practice at guessing the meaning of unfamiliar words. To help him when he gets stuck, footnotes translate those words that would have been given in English in earlier passages. By the time students have finished this lesson they are ready for one of the many available reading books that are equipped with footnotes or a glossary. With the help of a dictionary they can work their way through unedited materials.

There is nothing inevitable about the sequence by which I introduce the various aspects of French, but a few general principles seem fairly clear. First, other things being equal, one would want to introduce the most common and pervasive features first. We would like to introduce as much French as quickly as possible so as to give the passages a French "feel." Even a few high frequency words, for instance, can quickly convert a considerable proportion of the text to French and give the students a sense of satisfying progress. Second, however, we ought to capitalize on whatever organization we can find in the language and introduce related things together. This is why I introduced all the pronouns at the same time, even though some pronouns are by no means common. Third, if it does not conflict with other criteria, it may be helpful to introduce forms that help to support the overall structure of the language, particularly where this structure is quite different from the student's native language patterns. This is one criterion that led me to introduce the French person-number system very early. A fourth principle is to keep the increments within manageable proportions. This does not mean that we should progress by micro-steps, as in most "programmed" instruction, but we do not want to overwhelm the learner with too much at once. The French pronoun system is more complex than the English system, but it can still be introduced as a block. The verb system is so much more complex that it needs several lessons.

From the learner's point of view, the single most difficult challenge is to gain control over the masses of vocabulary of her new language. Different types of words, however, present different sorts of challenges. The meaning of so-called "content" words (nouns, in particular, but also many verbs and adjectives) is more difficult to guess from the context than is the meaning of "function" words (grammatical particles such as prepositions and conjunctions). The uses of these function words are often quite eccentric, and they are likely to be incommensurable from one language to another. This makes it very difficult to learn function words from a dictionary, and their use is so tightly bound up with the grammar of the language that they can hardly be learned except within a linguistic context. This makes the function words especially well-suited to being introduced within a full linguistic context, even if that context is largely made up of words from another language. Since the function words are very common, a reader has ample chance to see them used in a variety of circumstances, so she can absorb a firm sense of their usage. Mixed texts provide a rapid and relatively painless method by which students can gain a receptive grasp of the grammar and of the associated functional vocabulary of a language. The great mass of content words will, inevitably, take longer, but they will come most easily if the student has a firm grasp of the grammatical matrix formed by the morphology and the function words, for it is into this matrix that the content words fit.

Results

Students in a French reading course that met four hours a week had no difficulty working through my materials in nine weeks. By then they had read all of *Bonjour Tristesse* by Françoise Sagan, about half of *Les Carnets du Major Thompson* by Pierre Daninos, and four French magazine articles. This amounted to about 70,000 words and, even if only half of these words were French, this is considerably more than they could expect to work through in a more conventional class. They had been introduced to all the grammar they would need for reading French or even for understanding the spoken language, though they needed to expand their vocabulary and their under-standing of idioms, and they could hardly have identified every irregular verb form. After finishing the mixed language materials they used the remaining weeks of the term to read Georges Simenon's *Le Meurtre d'un Etudiant* (1971), a Maigret mystery in its full original form, except that it is equipped with a glossary and footnotes that define some vocabulary items and explain some idioms. At no time during the term had they been subjected to childishly easy material or been forced to struggle, painful word by painful word, through material that was much too difficult for them. They had reached the point where, with the help of a dictionary, they could read unprepared material. Within a single term they had gained a solid foundation for reading, and enjoyed themselves while doing so. Many students have passed the University of Michigan graduate reading examination in French after little more than work with my materials, although this may say more about the level of the examination than about the materials.

Advantages and Disadvantages

The method of mixed texts offers a number of striking advantages over other methods of early language instruction. Several of my students have told me that they became so caught up in the story they were reading, so eager to find out what was going to happen next, that they found it difficult to spend as much time on the grammar as they felt they should. In response, I have always told them that what really matters is their ability to understand what they read. The grammatical notes are provided only as a means of helping them find their way through the text, and if they can read with little attention to the notes, then so much the better. It is a rare language course that allows beginning students to become this engrossed in the content of their reading. A course that can motivate students to read, and spare them the tedium of childish materials deserves to be taken seriously even if it has little else to recommend it.

The method focuses much of the students' conscious attention on the area of language that is of greatest concern to the ordinary speaker: the meaning. Students must always read for understanding. Grammar is only a means to the end of extracting meaning. New words and new constructions are always learned in a familiar context and one can scarcely exaggerate the assistance the context provides. Languages are highly redundant. If enough of a text is understood, the final pieces can usually be guessed and, in general, the fuller the context, the more successful is guessing likely to be. Thus, the context provided by a connected text is far more helpful than that provided by an isolated sentence. If new words are only gradually introduced among predominantly familiar materials, the text used will always consist largely of familiar items, and many, or even most, of the new items can be guessed successfully. The reader will be less often forced to interrupt the story to flounder through the dictionary.

After encountering a new word several times in contexts where its meaning can be guessed, it would be nice to believe that its meaning will be learned so well that it can then become part of the context within which still other words can be learned. Sadly, words are not always so easily absorbed. It is possible to encounter a word repeatedly in contexts where its meaning is clear, and still not learn to recognize it in isolation, where it lacks the comforting support of a context. When using my French materials, some students relied so heavily on context that they managed to avoid absorbing a sufficient understanding of the gradually accumulating French terms. Finally, rather suddenly in some cases, the French accumulated to the point where the meaning of the sentences began to break down. The familiar context was no longer full enough to supply meaning to the unknown parts. At this point students have little choice but to go back and review, trying this time to get enough control of some of the accumulating vocabulary to continue comfortably. The considerable experience they will have had by then should at least ease the final mastery of these words.

I have already pointed out that the mixed language method allows a radical reordering of the sequence in which the aspects of the language are presented to students. Not only does it permit the student to start with the broadest patterns of the language, such as word order, but it also allows a much more systematic presentation of grammatical patterns than is possible in a course where the most urgent goal is to provide students with something to say.

There is room for widely differing opinions about the need, or even the usefulness, of laying out a grammatical system, such as that of the pronouns, in an abstract way. A language cannot, after all, be learned as if it is a system of logic. To some extent it must simply be taken in as an irregular, eccentric, and often illogical miscellany of facts. One of the insistent dilemmas of lesson design is to seek an optimum balance between an abstract intellectual approach that provides explicit rules and generalizations, and a more intuitive approach that relies on memory of specific facts. To the extent that abstract rules and generalizations are to be used at all, however, they would surely seem to be most useful for the broad and general aspects of the language. The irregular and eccentric details can be better abandoned to gradual absorption. All too often, however, students face precisely the opposite presentation. They are told, explicitly, about endless eccentricities and irregularities, such as the horrid spelling details of French irregular verbs, but the broader aspects of the language are never laid out with any clarity so that students come to perceive them only gradually through the murk of the details.

Sooner or later, of course, language learners must cope with the details and irregularities, but learning to recognize them is far easier than learning to produce them. Beginning students who are asked to speak or to write, must, if they are to avoid multiple errors, keep a hundred details in mind at the same time. If they do not need to produce the language, on the other hand, progress can be much more rapid, and if students finally decide they want to speak or write, their experience with hundreds of pages of the mature language will have given them a sense of the language, and even a few of its eccentricities will have come to seem natural—to "sound right."

The mixed language method has one final helpful feature. The changing proportions of the two languages in the text give the students a constant and visible measure of their progress. As the weeks go by, they can watch with satisfaction as the text shifts toward the new language. At every point they can see exactly how far they still have to go.

The advantages of the mixed language approach must be weighed against some obvious disadvantages. The most immediate problem is that the texts may seem unaesthetic. Those with a sensitive appreciation for the languages may find the language salad of the reading passages to be frivolous if not outright repellent. I feel that such a reaction deserves to be countered by pointing out that the childish materials we give to beginning students in most language courses have even fewer delights. If we are to worry about delicate sensitivities, we should surely worry most about the sensitivities of the students who must read the materials. Those who are already skilled in the languages and who find the teaching materials distasteful need not look at them. The students have no choice.

A different kind of problem lies in the enormous amount of work required to prepare the texts. A dreadful number of words must be indexed to make sure they are introduced consistently, and I have had no temptation to accede to kind student suggestions that I get busy and prepare materials in German and Russian. Still, the amount of work required is hardly a criticism of the method. If more work for the lesson designer results in less work for the students, that is surely a proper trade-off.

If used alone, however, the most obvious disadvantage of this method is that when students have finished, they can neither write nor engage in conversation. For many students the advantages of rapid progress in reading far outweigh the limitations on conversation. Other students would certainly prefer a course that promises progress in the spoken language as well.

This brings us to the question of whether students who have learned to read with mixed language materials will be handicapped if they later want to add a conversational ability to their repertory of skills. I cannot yet give a final answer to this question, but I have asked students who have used my materials how they feel about it, and the unanimous prognosis is that there would be few problems. It may be that if students invent their own pronunciations they will need some corrective relearning, but the feeling for structure, and the considerable stock of receptive vocabulary that reading provides, should allow them to make relatively rapid progress once they are motivated to work on the spoken language. Still, the method, by itself, is surely not sufficient for students who aspire to generalized language skills. It might, however, be used as one component of a more general course.

The mixed language reading method has one final and more serious problem: pronunciation. It shares this problem with any method that is confined to reading, particularly in a language like French where the orthography gives a poor representation of pronunciation. I have refrained from asking my students to pronounce anything at all in French, but now and then they mention French words, and it is apparent that their ideas about pronunciation can be quite wildly eccentric. Some students seem willing to read in happy ignorance of native pronunciation, even while admitting that they cannot refrain from inventing their own pronunciations for their own private use. Other students, however, feel distinctly uncomfortable when they do not know how the words are pronounced. They are bothered if they cannot subvocalize as they read, and some even want to be able to read aloud. I have offered such students two kinds of help.

First, I have provided them with a description of French pronunciation. More accurately, I have given them descriptions of how the letters of French are pronounced under varying circumstances. Students can refer to this when they feel they need help, but the relationship between French pronunciation and orthography is so complex, that this is hardly a satisfactory solution. Students with no exposure to the spoken language find it very difficult to use a written description.

My second method of helping students with pronunciation has been to record the text, French and English all mixed together, on tape. Students can then listen to the tape as they follow the written text on paper. At first I thought of this as little more than a joke, but it proved far easier and more natural to read the text aloud than I had expected. One has a certan problem with articulatory acrobatics as one repeatedly jumps back and forth from French to English pronunciation, but the reasonable solution to this difficulty is to aim for accurate French pronunciation and let the English words acquire a French quality if that makes the text easier to read. I asked a native French speaker to record some of the text for me and I was amused to find that as he read and as he grew accustomed to his task, his pronunciation of the English words became more and more heavily accented. If the intention is to give students a feeling for French pronunciation, the distortion of the English words would seem to be of little consequence.

Reading the mixed texts aloud proved less artificial than I had anticipated. When first inspected, the texts certainly look artificial, but when working through them in sequence it proves quite natural to read them as a coherent language. They can easily be given a natural intonation and, while one must slip rapidly back and forth between words of English and French origins, these meld together into a single communication system that soon loses its initial look of implausibility.

The real test of the tapes, however, is what they do for the students, and here I had a surprise. Students reported that hearing the tapes not only gave them a sense of what French sounds like and a sense of how the letters are related to the sounds, but also, by hearing the rhythm and intonation of the language, they gained a sense of its structure. The varying emphasis that readers gave to different words and the way they grouped their words into phrases made the passages considerably easier to understand than when students were limited to written texts alone. The recordings, therefore, seemed to offer a useful supplement to the written texts even for students who cared only about reading. The recordings also open the possibility of incorporating mixed texts into a language course with broader goals than simply reading, a possibility to which I will return.

I have often been asked how I would handle languages such as Russian that do not use the Roman alphabet, or, even worse, languages such as Arabic or Hebrew, in which the direction of writing is different from English. For Russian, I would be tempted to introduce the Cyrillic alphabet by first teaching students to read English that has been transcribed into Cyrillic. Once students feel comfortable with the alphabet it would seem possible to proceed much as I have done with French. It might be possible to teach Arabic and Hebrew orthography in the same way, but mixing right-to-left Arabic or Hebrew into the same passage with left-to-right English might pose insuperable problems. Since we read with a series of discrete fixations and not with a continuous sweep of our eyes, however, it might even be possible to mix words of different directions together in the same passage. At first sight, the possibilities for Chinese seem to be quite promising. Chinese characters could easily be sprinkled in among the English words in gradually increasing proportions. The reader might even vocalize the characters by means of English words. The method would make it difficult to capitalize upon the considerable phonetic component of the characters, however, and this might be a fatal drawback. The problems posed by different writing systems will only be clearly seen when experiments are made with practical lessons.

Oral and Written Language

I began my French experiment with the belief that those who wanted only to read deserved materials that would allow them to escape the multiple distractions of a general language course. I doubted that the spoken language had to be given its customary emphasis. Some of the students seemed to be content with nothing but reading. A few seemed to assign their own imaginative sounds to the letters they read, but they claimed no sense of deprivation at never hearing the language. Others, however, were left dissatisfied. Even without any special motivation to speak, they wanted to know how the language sounded. They wanted to be able to assign reasonable noises to the letters, words, and sentences they read.

We know almost nothing about what goes on beneath the level of consciousness when a language is acquired, but it is clear, at least, that we acquire many things without ever knowing that we are acquiring them. We absorb and come to use patterns about which we never gain conscious knowledge. Ideally, we ought to organize our language pedagogy in a way that would encourage whatever unconscious acquisition processes survive puberty, but we are groping in the dark as long as we do not know what these processes are or how they work. Perhaps, after all, unconscious processes of language acquisition depend in some degree, on aural reception. Since, in normal human beings, hearing is the first sensory system to be involved with language, it may turn out to play a special role in acquisition. This is not to deny the possbility of learning to read a language without ever hearing it. Some people do learn this way. But for some students, even for some of those whose goals are limited to reading, the time devoted to listening may pay off in the long run.

The taped recordings of the mixed texts helped some students more than I had expected and in ways that I had not anticipated. Not only did the students acquire a feeling for the sounds of the language, but they were also able to sense certain aspects of the grammatical structure that are carried more clearly by the intonation and the emphasis of the spoken language than by anything that appears in writing (see also Gary and Gary, 1980, 1981).

The help these students derived from the recordings of the mixed texts undermined my earlier confidence that the aural component of language instruction might be skipped entirely. On the other hand, the ease with which students got a feeling for the sounds of the language, even while concentrating on reading, raises the possibility that mixed texts might be incorporated into otherwise reasonably conventional classes. Almost any class could be made more interesting by using a few mixed texts. If texts could be adapted to various levels, simply by replacing the more esoteric words with English, it would be possible, at a much earlier stage of instruction for students to read materials of a level of interest appropriate to their own age. They would also be able to read far more rapidly, and this should be correspondingly satisfying. Mixed texts could easily be used in a class that gives heavier emphasis to the aural component of language than was given in my French course. The method is by no means restricted to classes where no other materials are used.

4

Aural Comprehension

How can students most expeditiously learn to understand the spoken language? What they certainly need, above all, is the chance to listen to massive amounts of the language in its natural, native form. Simply hearing the language is not enough; students must listen and understand; and they can be helped to understand if they hear the language spoken in contexts that provide maximum clues to meaning. A classroom provides a context of sorts. A teacher can exploit this context by pointing, gesturing, and assuming postures, and he can also judge the degree of student understanding and adjust his own language to the most useful level. Time in class is always limited, however; and as soon as we focus on comprehension, we must wonder if recordings might not relieve the teacher of some routine drill and, at the same time, ensure that all students hear the language as spoken by native speakers. With recordings, students should also be able to work at times of their own choosing. As countless dull commercial foreign language recordings and an even larger number of soporific language laboratory tapes demonstrate, however, the use of recordings is by no means enough to ensure the development of comprehension skills.

One trouble with many of the available recordings is the familiar insistence on production. Typical language laboratory tapes contain yawning gaps where students are supposed to repeat what they have heard and, with the more sophisticated programs, a student can even listen to a recording of her own voice. These tapes are designed with production rather than comprehension as the goal, and they constitute a stunning example of the productive bias of our pedagogy. Even recordings, manifestly best suited for helping with comprehension, are forced into a productive straightjacket.

Many available recordings also suffer seriously from the absence of any sensible context and from the lack of any easy feedback to the students about whether or not they have understood correctly. The mind's natural response to a long recorded passage that lacks context and that can only be murkily understood, is defiant rebellion. Anyone who has listened to typical language tapes will recall how dreadfully hard it is to keep the mind from wandering to more pleasant meadows. With the help of a dictionary, one can fight through the murk of a written text. There is no way to fight through the corresponding murk of a spoken text.

Equipment

At the University of Michigan we have constructed equipment, designed lessons, and recorded tapes that give students the flexibility of working on their own time and at their own speed, along with the advantages of hearing large amounts of the language as spoken by a native speaker.* Our tapes are designed with comprehension, rather than production, as the goal, and we believe they provide enough context and give the student enough control to overcome the limitations of a simple tape recorder and the tedium of most recorded language materials.

We provide our students with four crucial pieces of equipment: (1) a set of earphones through which they hear samples of the language; (2) pictures that provide a context for what is heard; (3) a set of controls for operating the equipment and for responding to what is heard; and (4) display lights that immediately tell the student whether or not each of his responses is correct. A student begins by selecting the tape cassette for the lesson that he wishes to study. He loads the cassette into the equipment and pushes the buttons that are needed to get things started. Typically, he then hears a few instructions that describe the form of the coming lesson and tell him which picture to look at. Then comes a sample of the language. This sample or "frame" may consist of a single word, a phrase, a sentence, or longer passage, but as soon as the frame is finished, the tape stops and waits for the student to

---

*Our Indonesian project is described in Burling et al., 1981, and more extensively in Burling and Becker, 1979.

react. Most often he must relate the language he has just heard to the picture he is looking at. In one typical lesson type, he hears a statement that may be either true or false of the picture in front of him. He must listen to the statement, look at the picture, and decide whether or not the statement correctly describes the picture.

The student can call for the frame to repeat as often as he wants, but once he has decided on his choice of "true" or "false," he pushes a button on his control pad. This is a set of buttons much like those on a pocket calculator or a slightly augmented pushbutton telephone. Several buttons are used for basic controls—starting, stopping, calling for repetitions, and so forth—but sixteen of the buttons (labeled on our present equipment as 0–9 and A–F) are possible "answers" to the frames. For true-false sentences, our convention has been that "1" means "true" and "2" means "false." Thus, when the student thinks he has heard a true sentence, he presses control button "1," but if he thinks his sentence is false, he must press "2" instead. The internal circuitry of the equipment then goes to work, though only the outcome is visible to the student. First, the display light tells the student whether or not he has made a correct choice. If his choice has been correct, he has the satisfaction of knowing this immediately. He can then push a button that calls for a new frame. He listens again and shows his understanding with another button push and, as long as he makes no mistakes, he can advance, frame by frame, through the tape.

If he makes a mistake, however, the display lights inform him of that sad fact, and when he nexts calls for another sample of the language he will not advance to a new frame, but instead will hear the old frame repeated. It will continue to repeat as long as the student continues to make mistakes, but when he finally gives the correct response immediately after having made one or more errors, the equipment rewinds the tape *two* frames. The mistake suggests the need for a bit of extra practice and the equipment responds automatically by providing that practice. The student must then try to get the previous frame correct; if he does, he will then advance once more to the frame where he made his mistake; he must get that one correct again, and only then will he finally be allowed to advance to an entirely new frame.

Since mistakes slow him down, the student is motivated to do his best to get the answers right, and what he needs, above all, is to understand. The student is consistently pushed to focus his attention on the meaning of what he hears. As the student concentrates on meaning, the phonology and grammar tend to recede to the background of his consciousness, for they are important only to the extent that they must be used to keep words distinct from one another and to organize the relations among words. Often, the details of phonology and grammar do not matter very much, but a student cannot possibly work through a lesson without understanding what he hears.

The most crucial factors in building listening comprehension are built into this equipment: the learner listens to a great deal of the language as spoken by a native speaker; he concentrates on meaning in a visible context provided by the pictures; he can call for as many repetitions as he wants; he has a constant and instantaneous check on whether or not he has understood correctly. Of course the equipment is a cold and impersonal machine of buttons and wires. The context provided by a set of pictures can never be as full or as interesting as the context in which language is used by real people in their daily lives. On the other hand, the equipment has compensating advantages: it never grows impatient; it is willing to repeat endlessly and without complaint; it speaks the language with impeccable pronunciation and flawless syntax.

Our "machine" as we have come to call it, has a complex internal anatomy. Students need be concerned only with its input and output—the tape well into which they load the cassettes, the earphones through which they hear samples of the language, the array of buttons with which they control the action, and the lights that tell them whether or not they are correct. The reader, however, deserves to know more about its construction.

At its heart are two essential pieces of equipment: a tape drive, and a microprocessor that carries messages between the tape drive, the signal lights, and the student. The tape drive must be a reliable one. It must, with confidence and precision, start, stop, go forward, and reverse, thousands upon thousands of times. If it works correctly 1,000 times, but errs on the 1,001st, the student's reaction can only be frustration and fury. Our equipment uses a Triple i "Super Deck" tape drive which has worked very well; however, technical developments are steadily accumulating in this area, and new and ever more versatile and reliable tape drives are likely to appear at regular intervals. Our microprocessor is a Kim-1, a standard microprocessor that has been widely used by hobbyists; once again, however, technical developments in this area are proceeding so rapidly that ever more versatile and ever less expensive devices are certain to become available each year.

A microprocessor is a genuine, though miniature, computer. When compared to a large computer, its capacities seem relatively limited, but it is far more versatile and powerful than a pocket calculator. Microprocessors also demand more specialized knowledge to program than does a pocket calculator, but they can be programmed to carry out a wide variety of routines. Ours was programmed to receive the answers punched into it by the student through its array of buttons, compare these answers with a table of correct answers supplied by the lesson designers, send the appropriate signal to the display lights to tell the student whether or not his answer is correct, and send instructions to the tape drive that tell it how to position itself for the next frame. It may instruct the tape drive to back up one frame (when the student makes an error), back up two frames (when the student makes a correct response after having made a mistake on the previous try), or advance to the next frame (when the student has made a correct response following a preceding correct response). The microprocesor is the part of the equipment that stores the table of correct answers, sorts out the signals, compares them, and, in accordance with the program supplied by the lesson designers, makes the decision about what the student needs next.

Conceptually, our system is far less complex than many of the interactive computer programs that are now becoming commonplace, but virtually all standard computer systems provide written output, either on a display screen or as "hard copy" disgorged by a printer of some sort. For teaching comprehension of a spoken language, however, we need an audio output of high quality. Since the technology of audio output has not been as intensively developed as the technology of printed output, we were forced to construct our own equipment. Our "machine" is unique, built in our language laboratory, and, at this writing, a long way from becoming a production model. This limits its relevance for anyone who might like to experiment with our methods, for it is not yet possible to go to a computer store and purchase equipment such as I describe. Nevertheless, both tape recorders and microprocessors are developing rapidly, and equipment that will accomplish what we require will almost surely become widely available in the next few years. This makes it worthwhile to describe in some detail the uses to which such equipment can be put.

Lesson Design

The first real trial for our machine was with a class in elementary Indonesian. In addition to building the equipment, of course, we had to design lessons, and in some respects this "software" development has been an even more exacting task than the building of the "hardware." We wanted our lessons to start at the beginning, and to build complexity gradually. We wanted to avoid translations as much as possible, but we thought we could provide a context in which meaning could be inferred from pictures. Instead of relying on translation, students would grasp the meaning by relating the language samples directly to the nonlinguistic context of the pictures. We wanted to encourage the students to form their own hypotheses about the workings of the language, and we wanted them to be able to check their guesses by listening to many examples and discovering whether or not they understood them correctly. At the same time, we very much wanted the lessons to be fun. We were acutely aware that our equipment was a cold piece of hardware, not a warm human being, and we wanted to do our best to keep the lessons from becoming mechanical and dull.

We have developed several different types of lessons. The simplest to design, but least interesting to use, is to give the student a picture with about ten numbered objects and let her hear the names of these objects through her earphones. The student hears a word, decides which picture it names, and punches the button on the touch pad that carries the number of that picture. Every time she gets a word right, she is given another example, but whenever she makes a mistake, she hears the word again. We used the picture shown in Figure 1, for instance, to introduce the names of the objects most likely to be found on an Indonesian dining table. Simple sketches like this are entirely adequate for our purposes, although, as can be seen, we did try to let them convey something of the look of Indonesia.

A lesson like this offers a quick and easy introduction to a series of words, but it is anything but imaginative. It amounts to little

Figure 1

more than the auditory equivalent of a word list or a bundle of
flash cards, although it does seem better to help the student form
a direct association between a visible object and a sound than
between a written Indonesian word and a written English word,
in the way that word lists and flash cards so insidiously encourage.

Mere memorization of vocabulary should not go on too long,
and once the words begin to be more or less recognizable, more
imaginative lessons can be used to consolidate them in memory.
One pattern that students have found interesting is the one
already mentioned, which consists of sentences that are either
true or false of a general scene that shows the objects just
studied. The vaguely surrealistic scene shown in Figure 2 was
given to students to help them consolidate the names for the
objects shown in the picture, and for certain relationships among
them, and to give further practice with some numbers. The lesson
included the Indonesian equivalents for such sentences as the
following: "There are five chairs" (false). "There are three fish"
(false). "There are two bananas in the basket" (true). "One cat is on

Figure 2

the table" (true). "A cat is in the tree" (false). "There are two coconut trees and one banana tree" (true). "Three fish are on a plate" (true). Obviously the lesson designers could provide as many sentences of this type as they wanted. Ideally there should be enough to consolidate the vocabulary but not so many as to induce boredom.

As a slight variant of the true-false lesson we sometimes asked yes-no questions. The questions often asked something about a pictured scene and the student would have to push button 1 if the answer was "yes" and button 2 if it was "no." Such a lesson, of course, gives realistic practice with question forms as well as with the more specific vocabulary of the lesson.

All the sentences used in such lessons, false as well as true, are, of course, grammatically well formed, and all are spoken by a native speaker of Indonesian. All provide good examples of the language, but students must concentrate not on the form of the sentences but upon their meaning, and they must decide whether or not they correspond to the situation in the picture. By concentrating on meaning, the student's attention is always focused where ordinary speakers of the language focus their attention.

True-false sentences and yes-no questions have one obvious defect. Half the time the students can get a correct answer simply by guessing, and they can always get the right answer on the second try even without understanding what went wrong the first time. A lesson pattern with only two possible answers to each frame allows students to guess their way through the tape without understanding and without learning very much. Students always find it more interesting to understand the sentences, so they have little desire to resort to blind guessing; but it does seem best to supplement true-false lessons with lesson patterns that offer enough alternative answers to make guessing unprofitable.

In some lessons we increased the alternatives available to the students by giving them multiple-choice questions or "fill in the blank" type sentences with several possible answers. We might, for instance, use such questions as this: "Where is the cat? (1) on the table; (2) under the table; (3) beside the table." Students would have to understand the questions and the alternative answers and make their selections with reference to the picture. Or the student might hear "Mr. Suleiman is (1) getting on the bus; (2)

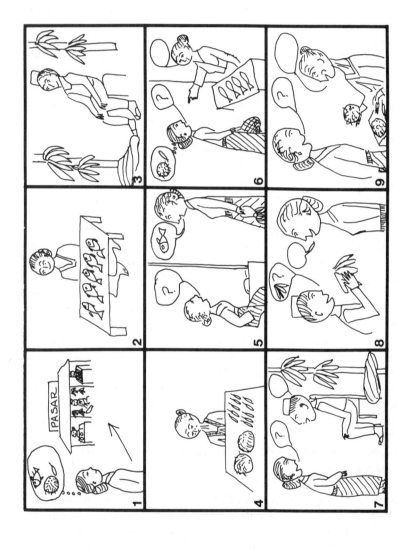

Figure 3

getting off the bus; (3) waving to the crowd." Again, they would have to understand each of the alternatives so as to reject the wrong ones and select the correct answer.

In order to offer the students more variety and open the possibility of a still larger number of alternatives, we also developed lessons that had a series of pictures like a familiar comic strip. Such a series can show a connected sequence of events or a story. We even used a number of comic strip conventions: word balloons that show which characters are speaking, or a series of bubbles leading to a character that show what someone is thinking. Our balloons, however, were either empty or filled with a picture instead of written words. We supplied the words through the earphones.

Figure 3 shows a series of pictures in which Mrs. Suleiman, a character who has been previously introduced, is seen going to the market, speaking with shopkeepers, and making her purchases. The student hears sentences such as these: "Mrs. Suleiman is going to the market" (1). "Mrs. Suleiman wants to buy fish, a coconut, and chile peppers" (1). "This is Mrs. Minah; she sells fish at the market" (2). "Would you like to buy bananas ma'am? No thank you, I don't want any" (8). As the examples show, it is possible for several sentences to correspond to a single picture, and the range and complexity of the sentences is limited only by the imagination of the designer. The student hears a frame and must decide which picture it is related to. As with the other types of lessons, a correct choice brings a new example while an incorrect choice results in a repetition.

Lessons of this sort can be interesting for the student, and they have the virtue of allowing sequence and continuity to be conveyed. Intention and time relationships are more easily introduced than with individual pictures. These lessons do raise certain problems for the designer, however. It is difficult to plan pictures that are clearly distinct and to write sentences that unambiguously refer to just one single picture in the way that our equipment demands. If a sentence is made sufficiently long and complex to be unambiguous in its referent, there is a risk that students will learn to associate it with the correct picture, but for irrelevant reasons. They may notice something tangential or irrelevant about the sentence and learn to recognize it in that way without really understanding it adequately.

Our early lessons usually begin with a brief set of instructions in English, but as the students' capacities increase, the instructions, as well as the lesson itself, are given in Indonesian. The pictures and the recordings of our early lessons are augmented, in some later lessons, with a written portion. We experimented with lessons in which a story was given both in a recorded form and in writing, so that the students could both see and hear what they were trying to understand, and in a few cases we gave alternative answers in written form—each with a number—to questions they heard on the tape. The possible lesson patterns that could be devised are almost endless.

With sufficient ingenuity, it would be possible to introduce virtually every aspect of the language, both lexical and syntactic, by means of pictures and the associated recorded samples of the language. One would have to start with "pictureable" phenomena. The names of visible objects, and easy-to-picture actions and qualities such as *walk, stand up, eat, black,* and *big* come most easily. Spacial relationships such as those conveyed by English prepositions are easy to introduce with pictures, but time relationships pose more difficulties, just as they do for first language learners. By means of sequences of pictures, however, even the meaning of words that indicate time relationships can be conveyed. We were able to introduce Indonesian auxiliary verbs that indicate such abstract concepts as completed action and intention, for instance, by means of a sequence of pictures that formed a story. We also used pictures of clocks and calendars to introduce some of the more specific vocabulary of time.

In designing lessons, however, there is considerable temptation to stretch ingenuity beyond the point of corresponding utility. Since children learn monolingually, by hearing their mother tongue in situations where they can associate what they hear with the events around them, it is tempting to rely on the same strategy with our equipment. Our pictures must substitute for the situation in which a child hears his first language, but in both cases the language can be built up, step by step and in parallel ways. Such a course is not impossible, but it can be slow and tortuous.

The limitation that is inherent in any system that makes extensive use of pictures is that many words can be pictured only with great difficulty, or hardly at all. Consider the immediately preceding sentence, for instance; a perfectly ordinary sentence, but one that would be difficult to convey in a picture. The word "picture" itself might be conveyed visually, and the purely grammatical words such as "the," "of," and "is" would have appeared so early and so often in any set of lessons and in such close association with "pictureable" words that their meanings might be easily inferred. A large block of words remains, however, that could be introduced through pictures only with great difficulty: "limitation, inherent, system, difficulty, hardly." Children require many long years to master all this vocabulary. They must slowly infer the meaning of some of the words from their contexts, and for some words they receive explicit definitions in response to the incessant questions of childhood: "Daddy, what does 'system' mean?" "What does 'inherent' mean?" This long process of building up the vocabulary of one's native language takes many years of immersion. The foreign language student is never eager to take so much time.

Sooner or later, therefore, students of foreign languages and their teachers always resort to translation. Translation allows many problems to be chopped through easily, and the price of avoiding it is unreasonably high. Too much translation that comes too soon can convey the misleading impression that the new language amounts to some peculiar and complex transformation of the student's native language, instead of being an independent system in its own right. But too little translation condemns the student to endless guessing through endless murky mysteries. Setting the balance between translation on the one hand and direct association of the language with experience and context on the other is an important point of artistry required of anyone who would design foreign language teaching materials.

Our equipment allows an important segment of language to be introduced and understood with no reliance on translation. This can provide students with a solid core of the language and a solid sense that this new language really has its own system and is not simply a strange and distorted incarnation of English. Early in their course of study, students can have the experience of understanding complex passages, spoken at natural speeds that move fast enough to make it impossible for them to translate into their own language. They must understand the language directly. There remain other aspects of the language that are less easily introduced in this way, and for these aspects other techniques can usefully complement our methods.

Results, Problems, and Prospects

I cannot offer results of our Indonesian program that would satisfy a statistically minded experimentalist. The students who studied Indonesian with our equipment were too few and too heterogeneous for the results to be statistically meaningful. But I can offer impressions, and I feel particularly qualified to do so because I was one of the first to use the equipment and try the method. I was the only member of the team that organized the Indonesian program who had never before studied Indonesian, and this made me the natural first guinea pig. Throughout the first year I worked through the lessons along with the enrolled students, and I regularly discussed the project with them. Their reactions were enough like mine to give me confidence that my own reactions were not simply idiosyncratic.

The first reaction can be given with confidence: our initial fear that the equipment would seem mechanical, tyrannical, and coldly impersonal was not borne out. Instead, the students and I enjoyed fiddling with the machine and working through the lessons. During the first year we were still working some mechanical bugs out of the system, and we had a number of frustrating breakdowns. Anyone tempted to toy with experimental electronic equipment should be warned that it can have an eerie tendency to act as if it had a mind of its own. During the first few months our sensitive machine now and then picked up stray electrical static through its power cord and arbitrarily interpreted it as a signal to back up, or fast forward, or perform various other unwanted maneuvers. We gradually taught it to behave, however, and when it did so, it was fun to use.

The equipment allows the students a welcome degree of flexibility. They can use it at times of their own choosing, and can select any lesson from the rack of tapes. They can repeat as often as they want. We refrained from offering our students precise instructions about how to proceed because we wanted to learn what they found most helpful, and they turned out to vary considerably in their styles. Some took a good many notes and wrote down what they heard; others seemed content to listen without writing. Some listened in silence; a few seemed impelled to mumble and repeat everything they heard. It seemed to us that the flexibility allowed by the equipment was a considerable virtue, for it allowed each student to adapt the equipment to her or his own learning style. We tried not to spy on the students while they were using the equipment because we wanted them to feel free to make mistakes with no threat of scorn or disapproval. We wanted them to feel free to repeat, without embarrassment, as often as they wanted.

In the course of an hour with the equipment students hear more of the language than they would hear in any but the most exceptional classroom. The language is interrupted only by pauses while the listeners think about what they have heard, by short rewindings of the tape, and by an occasional break for changing to a new lesson. Everything heard, of course, is spoken by a native speaker. None of us found an hour with the equipment to be too long, and some could work with it happily for as long as two hours.

Nobody who works with our equipment can cling for long to the idea that comprehension, in any meaningful sense, is "passive." Rather, it requires hard, concentrated work. The listeners must attend carefully, think hard about the words they hear, grope to understand what these words refer to, and exercise all their ingenuity to guess the meaning of the phrases, sentences, paragraphs, and conversations built from the words. But the hard work of listening and thinking about what is heard can also be fun. It is like working through an intricate puzzle that invites solution—learners must be willing to make mistakes and learn by them; they will then be rewarded by flashes of understanding as their first murky guesses are replaced by growing comprehension. Learning to understand a language is an active, creative process. It requires that students play their hunches, form hypotheses, and test their guesses with new examples, even if they never open their mouths to say anything in the language at all.

After one listens to samples of the foreign language for an hour, required at every turn to demonstrate understanding of what has been heard, the language begins to echo in one's head. Even with no direct pressure to reproduce the language, listeners find themselves repeating things inwardly. The long experience of listening builds up to an extensive knowledge of the language, and to a sense of what sounds right. During the first term we worked with our equipment we had almost no explicit instruction in either syntax or phonology. At the beginning of the second term, when we first began to use the language productively, our pronunciation showed no serious problem at all, and the syntax we were progressively expected to use seemed transparently easy. The phonology of Indonesian, to be sure, is relatively simple, and the syntax required at the elementary stages of the language is also fairly straightforward. Before offering a definitive judgment, our method should be tried with languages having more demanding phonology (e.g., Chinese) and more demanding syntax (e.g., Arabic). Nevertheless, our tentative conclusion is that our initial assumptions have been borne out; if comprehension is emphasized at the beginning, much of the phonology and syntax can be expected gradually to take care of themselves.

Phonology and syntax posed few problems as we worked to build our receptive ability of Indonesian; this left vocabulary as the major challenge. Words were what we needed to understand if we were to understand the sentences; words were what we were in danger of forgetting. The most urgent aspect of lesson design is to help the student, as quickly as possible, to recognize an increasing range of vocabulary.

Many of us who worked through the lessons had unexpected experiences which deserve to be noted, even if we cannot account for them fully. We found that we could often understand a sentence we heard even when we failed to understand all its parts. To some extent, this is a simple matter of redundancy—we did not need to understand everything, since so much in any language is repeated two or three times. But our experience seemed to rest on something else as well. We had the sense that we were leaping directly through the language to the meaning.

When we hear our own native language spoken, we attend to the meaning. We are rarely conscious of the particular phonological forms or syntactic patterns that are being used, and we may hardly even notice the particular words. The entire formal apparatus of the language becomes so transparent that we feel in direct contact with the message. As we worked with our tapes we began to hear the Indonesian message coming through almost as clearly—directly and with little awareness of the distracting screen of syntax and phonology. It was a rather wonderful if somewhat mysterious experience, something none of us had experienced before in the first term of a foreign language class.

Our initial trials with our equipment were sufficiently successful to encourage us to continue development. Students can work through a remarkably bulky volume of material in a term. It takes a great deal of labor to produce the lessons, but they allow a student, quite rapidly, to build up an ability to comprehend the language.

The method did leave some students dissatisfied in a way we had not anticipated, however. Some of them would have liked written material along with the aural material they were hearing. Their wish, however, goes against the suggestions of some scholars who have developed comprehension approaches to language instruction. They argue that reading ability follows automatically the ability to understand the spoken language. If this is true, as it seems to be (at least for languages with familiar alphabets), there is no need to begin reading immediately. It has even been argued that early exposure to writing can be damaging, since misleading spelling causes students to draw incorrect inferences about pronunciation (Asher, 1972; Asher, Kusudo, and de la Torre, 1974; Winitz, 1973). Transfer from aural skills to reading is clear. Transfer from reading to aural skills is not.

By the time Americans embark on the study of Indonesian, however, they are already highly literate. College students, even high school students, have become so accustomed to learning by means of the written word that a purely aural approach can be disorienting. Literate adults come to think of their language as consisting of letters as much as it consists of sounds. Words become marks on paper rather than noises. Knowledge comes to be more easily absorbed through the eyes than through the ears. One student said to me, "It would be nice to have something on paper that I could carry around with me and review at odd moments—perhaps a card to stick onto my mirror to review while shaving."

It may be, moreover, that reading, or at least some written support for what the student is hearing, can offer shortcuts that will speed up the learning process. Mixed language texts such as those described in Chapter 3 can very quickly give students a sense of the overall organization of the language, introducing them to the full range of the grammar and allowing them to move quickly beyond graded materials. The ease of defining words on paper may even help comprehension of the spoken language to expand rapidly. Having words surrounded by white space, as on paper, instead of blurring into each other, as in spoken language, makes it much easier to sort out a written text, and students can far more quickly reach the kinds of complex adult texts that interest them. Thus, even though it may be true that aural skills are readily transferred to reading, some aural skills may be more efficiently acquired with the support of writing.

No appeal to the experience of first language learners can obscure the fact that our second language learners are highly literate. Written language is central to their lives and, for many of them, learning can proceed more expeditiously when it is supported by writing.

Thus, one conclusion I draw from our experiment with Indonesian is curiously complementary to one I drew from my experiment with French reading. Just as some students are helped to read if given some aural support for what they see on paper, so students can also be helped to understand the spoken language if given some written support. Much can be learned through the ears, but many adults learn more quickly if they have something to hold in their hands and see with their eyes. A program that combines instruction in aural comprehension with instruction in reading allows the eyes and ears to work together, and it might provide the most rapid progress of all.

Encouraging Comprehension

In the last two chapters I described two unorthodox techniques for helping people understand foreign languages. Both techniques have been tried with reasonable success, but they are only two of many possible methods of encouraging comprehension. In this chapter I propose, more briefly, a number of modifications, revisions, and additions to these two methods. Several might be used together in a general effort to help people learn to understand. Some of the methods I propose have been tried extensively by other experimenters, and I refer the reader to their own fuller descriptions of their work. I have tried out other methods more briefly, and the ideas offered here are intended to be more suggestive than definitive. I hope they may encourage a wide variety of experiments.

All my proposals, of course, are for ways of encouraging comprehension, but within that limitation they are meant to be as varied as possible. The grimmest aspect of a language class is boredom, and the more varied the materials used, the more likely the students are to profit.

The Monolingual Demonstration

The linguist Kenneth Pike has developed a public performance he calls the "monolingual demonstration." He is introduced, frequently in the presence of several hundred spectators, to a speaker of a language he has never before heard. In the course of an hour and a half, without using any common language, he demonstrates how much he can learn about the language from this speaker (Pike, 1967:29–30, 34–35, 225).

Pike usually brings along a few props, often some leaves, branches, and pebbles, and he may begin by holding them up and hoping that his informant will name them. He first learns the words for a few objects and then, with the help of gestures, learns how these words are used in short phrases and sentences: "big leaf, small leaf, big stone, this stone, that stone, I have a stone," etc. By assuming various postures he learns such expressions as "sit down, stand up, walk, yawn, give, take," and he is soon able to combine these with subject and object pronouns. Once the speaker has the idea of assigning names, it is easy to learn the words for body parts. These in turn invite the use of possessive pronouns. Within ninety minutes Pike can usually elicit and understand complex sentences that involve extensive modification and subordination, and he may have elicited well over a hundred words that sample every part of speech.

The monolingual demonstration has an almost magical quality. Usually the spectators have never before heard a word of the language, but they can easily follow the demonstration. They can understand the meanings of the words they hear, get an idea of the sound patterns, and at least glimpse the major patterns by which the words of the language are joined together into phrases and sentences. By the end of the demonstration, the members of the audience are astonished at how much they have understood.

I can imagine no better way to begin a foreign language class than with a monolingual demonstration. It starts where students start—from the beginning; it demands no overt response; it conveys a sense that understanding can develop rapidly; it avoids dependence on the native language; it introduces a good many words. Most of the words will not be clearly remembered after a single session, of course, but they will be more easily recognized when they appear in other contexts in the weeks that follow. The demonstration is also excellent theater.

In his monolingual demonstration Pike always works with a language he knows nothing about. A language teacher who wants to offer her students something similar to the demonstration has both the advantages and disadvantages that come with prior knowledge. Her knowledge may allow her to avoid chasing down dead ends, but it may also tempt her to move more rapidly than the students can follow. The beauty of Pike's demonstration is that his own difficulties and misunderstandings impose limits on the speed with which he can move. He is automatically held to an understandable speed. The spectator realizes how much can be learned in an hour and a half, even when starting from zero.

The monolingual demonstration has two virtues for beginning students. First, since it is monolingual, it avoids all dependence on the native language of either demonstrator or audience, and students quickly gain a sense of the independence of the new language from their old language. Second, it is utterly dependent on meaning. From the start of their training the students grasp the idea that words and sentences refer to objects, qualities, and events in the world. From the start, they avoid the need for translation and, instead, derive the meaning from the relation of the language to its context.

The Total Physical Response

Since the mid-1960s James Asher has pioneered a technique he calls the "Total Physical Response," and the reader should refer to his writings for a fuller description. (See especially Asher, 1977, *Learning Another Language Through Actions.*) Asher asks the teacher to use the new language in a way that calls for a physical rather than a verbal response from the students. By gestures and actions the teacher demonstrates what words and expressions mean, and then makes requests and issues commands of various sorts. The students must then demonstrate by their actions that they understand what they have been told to do. Starting with simple directions such as "Stand up!" "Sit down!" and "Turn around!" the teacher leads up to increasingly complex instructions such as "Rita, put your hand on the table," "Run with Miako to the door and jump," and "In one minute, Alfredo is going to sweep the floor." Students are not pushed to speak before they are ready, but they hear a great deal of the language. In all cases they must act out some physical activity, and Asher shows great ingenuity in incorporating a wide variety of grammar and vocabulary into the statements and commands students hear. Correct performance is impossible without understanding, and the students' total linguistic effort is directed toward comprehension of the meaning. They do not have to face the unnerving task of forming sentences of their own.

With sufficient ingenuity, it is possible to introduce a large vocabulary and a wide range of constructions in this way, and Asher believes that the physical activity of carrying out the tasks helps to fix the words and constructions in the minds of the students. The method has a great deal to recommend it, particularly during the first few weeks of a foreign language class, and the research results reported by Asher and his colleagues (summarized conveniently in Asher, 1977, pp. 3–36) constitute a convincing demonstration of its superiority over the more traditional audiovisual methods with which it has been compared.

One possible reservation concerns the willingness of mature students to act out the commands, but surely these activities are less painful than the pattern practice drills to which so many students have been subjected; in fact, Asher reports that even mature students engage happily in this method. Asher places great weight on the actual physical, kinesthetic response as a way to fix the language in memory; but apart from the gymnastics, his method has the profound virtue of consistently focusing on meaning, of always using the language within a context, of always emphasizing comprehension, and of regularly requiring students to demonstrate comprehension in ways other than by talking. Possibly these factors, as much as the physical response itself, explain Asher's success, and if these factors can be preserved through other means, the physical activity might to some extent be played down. Certainly Asher's methods deserve a place among the techniques by which students can be helped to understand.

Pictures

Our Indonesian experiment described in Chapter 4 made extensive use of pictures to avoid translation into the students' native language, and, apart from the special equipment our methods require, there are many ways that pictures can be used to provide a context for language. Valerian Postovsky's early experiments in comprehension training (1970) used equipment that projected four pictures onto a screen. The student heard a word or sentence and had to choose the picture that best fitted what he heard. As soon as he indicated his selection he would find out whether or not he had understood correctly. Winitz and Reeds (1975) developed a similar system for teaching German. More recently, Winitz and his associates have developed a sequence of many hundreds of pictures that dispenses with the four-way choices of his earlier experiments. The students simply look at a picture and listen to a word or sentence associated with it, and then move on to the next picture and next language sample (Winitz, 1981b). This type of program is far simpler to design than one that requires choices, but students still seem able to build up an extensive understanding of the language by associating the picture with what they hear.

James Nord and his associates have developed still another program based on pictures and audio input, but their students respond in a different way. Nord uses special latent image paper which is treated in such a way that only when students select the correct answer does a previously invisible sign appear that confirms their choice. Instead of the control light we use on our mechanical equipment, the student's choice is confirmed by a simple mark on his work sheet (Nord, 1980; Ingram, Nord, and Dragt, 1975).

Pictures help students to form direct links between their new language and the objects and events of the world that are portrayed in the pictures, so they help them escape excessive translation or excessive dependence on their native language. The chief limitation of pictures comes from the limitations in the imagination of the lesson designer. It is possible, and therefore tempting, to use pictures to introduce even quite abstract concepts, but words like *certain, occur,* and *misconception* can only be introduced with pictures at the price of considerable ingenuity and struggle on the part of both lesson designer and student. Finally, there comes a point where the dangers of too much translation are counterbalanced by the quick and easy solutions it provides. Our experience with pictures (like that of Postovsky, Winitz, and Nord) strongly supports their use in the early stages of comprehension instruction. Among other things, they allow students to work on their own, without the direct guidance of a teacher. But there is no need to fall into the trap of supposing that every resort to the students' native language is dangerous. Second language students already have a vast number of concepts and a vast number of labels for these concepts in their first language, and it is foolishly obsessional to refuse to exploit all this knowledge when it can speed up the process of learning the new labels of the new language.

Listening and Reading Together

My experiment with French reading seems to have suffered from insufficient aural support. On the other hand, our mechanized

Indonesian lessons suffered from insufficient written support. A program in which the eyes and ears can work together might avoid the pitfalls of both.

In preparation for a year in Sweden I learned to read and understand a good deal of Swedish by a method simple enough to be available to anyone who can find (1) a book in the language that he wants to learn and that has been translated into his own language, (2) the translation of the book to use as a pony, (3) a tape recorder, (4) a bilingual dictionary, and (5) a cooperative speaker of the language. I persuaded a Swedish speaker to read several hundred pages of my Swedish book into a tape recorder. I then listened to the recording at the same time that I read the book, giving my eyes and ears a chance to work together, and I found that I could understand more easily in that way than when limited either to the recording or to the written text alone. I used the English translation and, when necessary, the dictionary, to give me the meanings of words and idioms that I did not know or that I could not guess from the context. The translation was especially helpful when I had to sort through particularly difficult passages and complex constructions.

I usually began by listening to a passage two or three times straight through, trying to understand as much as I could without the help of the dictionary or translation. Then I would work through the passage more carefully, looking up unguessable but necessary words and figuring out mysterious constructions. Finally, I listened to the passage several more times, sometimes with the book in front of me and sometimes without it, but always with the goal of finally being able to put the book aside and listen to the recording straight through while understanding it completey.

Listening to a recording as one reads can be recommended on several grounds. First, of course, pronunciation is constantly impressed upon one's mind. We are much less likely to invent spelling pronunciations, to articulate silent letters, or resort to the pronunciation conventions of our own languages if we hear ample amounts of the language as spoken by a native speaker. Second, the reader's intonation gives important clues to the syntactic structure. A fluent reader groups the words and provides emphasis in a way that shows clearly which words belong together and which belong to separate phrases. The strings of words that appear in print are given an orderly relationship by the spoken intonation. Third, but possibly most important, listening to a recording forces learners to move so rapidly that translation into their native language is impossible. They can stop to look up words in the dictionary or to check the pony, but if they are to understand the recording they must learn to do so directly. They must understand the foreign language as it comes racing by. Of course a tape allows a passage to be heard again and again, but each time it will be heard at natural speed.

As with a monolingual demonstration, there is an almost magical quality about listening to a passage until it is fully understood. After some effort, the passage becomes transparent. The structure of the language, its sounds, and even its individual words are forgotten as one comes into direct contact with the meaning.

The method worked extremely well for one highly motivated learner—me. Just how well it would work on a large scale for an average class of mixed motivation and mixed abilities is difficult to predict. Many students might stop listening to a passage after one or two quick passes. A few might be tempted to omit the recording entirely and rely only on the reading. A few I am afraid, might even be content to limit their attention to the pony. We face a vulgar but familiar problem: How do we make sure that our students do enough work to learn the lesson?

Quizzes are the traditional answer. Passages that are similar but not identical to the passages they had worked through could be read to students, and they would have to demonstrate their understanding by such devices as judging the truth or falsity of the statements. If the quizzes reflect the materials of the studied passages, they might not only measure the students' progress but also motivate them to study their next lesson more thoroughly.

As I studied Swedish, grammar gave me few problems. This was, to be sure, partly because Swedish grammar shares so much with English, but even where Swedish grammar deviates sharply from any language I had studied earlier, it came with ease. Nor did pronunciation present recognition problems. Swedish pronunciation has an ample share of exotic features, but I listened to the language for many long hours, and became thoroughly familiar with its sounds before I made any serious attempt to pronounce them.

Vocabulary, however, was a problem from the beginning. I spent long hours looking up unknown words in my pony, and, when my pony was not sufficiently literal, I chased the words down in my dictionary. This is uninspiring work, and it might quickly discourage the weakly motivated. Students in a formal class deserve enough assistance to cut down the dictionary thumbing.

If listening-reading materials were to be prepared for a class, it should be a straightforward task to provide translations of the words that the student cannot yet be expected either to know or to guess from the context. These unkown words might even be divided into two classes. Students could be advised to pass over the rarer words for the moment, without any attempt to memorize them. The more common words could be marked in a way that would tell the student to bear down on them. Rare words, for instance, might be translated interlinearly, while the words the students should try to learn could be translated in the margins. In that way students could concentrate their efforts in areas most likely to be of immediate use, and they would avoid squandering their time either with fumbling through a dictionary or with the effort to memorize exotic vocabulary. If enough individual words are translated, a full translation of the text might not be essential, but, especially at the beginning, a pony would still be a great comfort. It could be used to escape from otherwise hopeless muddles with structure, and it would give students the confidence that they could fight through anything at all. Students should certainly be encouraged to do their best to figure things out for themselves before resorting to their pony, but endless puzzlements are of profit to no one.

As I was studying Swedish, a friend, an expert in language pedagogy, suggested that simultaneous listening and reading is an odd, even unnatural, activity. It is hardly a typical use of language, and it struck him as an unnatural way to learn. If one thinks of it either as a way of helping reading skills develop or as a way of encouraging comprehension of the spoken language, however, it may seem less strange. If one's goal is to learn to read, hearing the text read aloud helps sort out the aspects of the structure that are not well represented in the orthographic system. If one's goal is to learn to understand the spoken language, on the other hand, written transcriptions of the oral passages allow one to sort more easily through the confusing noises, to separate words from each other, and, when necessary, to look words up in the dictionary. The combined experience can be a shortcut to either goal.

Combining reading with listening as a means of helping students understand has received remarkably little attention, probably because comprehension, in general, has not been taken as seriously as it deserves. George Scherer (1950, 1952) advocated listening as a means of helping students with their reading, and he recognized the help that listening gives in sorting out the grammatical organization. But Scherer wrote at a time when audiolingual methods were becoming dominant, and his advice seems to have fallen on deaf ears. More recently Gary and Gary (1980), writing about the research of Nermine Fahmy (1979), report "Fahmy demonstrated that reading comprehension is significantly improved in the presence of aural accompaniment compared to reading without aural accompaniment." Similarly, J. P. Mooijman, in Holland, has advocated reading and listening together, and has reported highly encouraging results (personal communication). My own recommendation would be that, until students are so proficient that they can read their new language faster than the normal speed of the spoken language, they listen to recorded versions of everything they read. This will make it easier for them to understand the passages; it will force them to read too quickly to allow translation; it will help new vocabulary become fixed in their minds; and it will discourage outlandish pronunciations. With the modern ease and simplicity of cassette recordings, there is no longer any practical reason to deny students this help.

Rapid Colloquial Styles

The written form of most languages differs in a good many ways from the spoken form and, in particular, the written form is usually somewhat fuller. It represents a more abstract or more formal linguistic level of the language than is usually heard casually on the lips of speakers. When a written text is read aloud, the resulting style is likely to be substantially different from the most colloquial spoken style, and one of the most difficult challenges of language pedagogy is to help students understand this most colloquial oral style, especially in a conversation among two or more native speakers. The awful trouble that even the best students often have when finally forced to cope with the onslaught of rapid colloquial language has been noted repeatedly (e.g., Belasco, 1971a, 1971b).

One important way in which colloquial speech differs from the more formal styles is that speakers modify, contract, elide, or delete many of the features that appear in the underlying forms. Many of these features are more regularly represented in writing, and they even show up in careful reading style. In addition, of course, the spoken style is set apart from the written form of the language by its own words, idioms, and grammatical patterns.

Adults often find it very difficult to learn the fast speech rules and the informal vocabulary and idioms of the most colloquial style. It is striking, for instance, that adult learners often find children particularly difficult to understand. Children use a relatively restricted vocabulary and even a somewhat limited range of grammatical constructions. We might expect this to make children relatively easy to understand, but it does not. The problem must be that, however limited children's language may be in certain respects, it is not at all limited in its use of fast speech rules or in the most colloquial level of vocabulary, idiom, and syntax. Children may not even be able to shift out of this style. The colloquial level, represented both by the speech of children and by rapid adult chatter, is often out of a foreigner's range.

Gillian Brown (1977) has given us a careful analysis of the phonological differences between relatively formal spoken English and one fast colloquial British dialect, along with recommendations for teaching comprehension of the fast colloquial. She shows just how different the phonology of formal and informal dialects can be, and shows the problems these differences can pose to a learner. She advocates instruction in comprehending fast colloquial speech without any insistence at all upon production. She recognizes that learners can make themselves understood quite satisfactorily without actively using the fast speech rules of fluent speakers, but they cannot escape from hearing them.*

---

*I admire Brown's analysis of the phonological characteristics of fast colloquial English, and I admire her diagnosis of the problem, but I believe her cure may be a bit more extreme than necessary. She proposes deliberate step by step instruction in various aspects of fast speech; but I suggest that relatively simple recordings, together with transcripts, could more quickly and easily allow students to build up a sense of the equivalences among the styles than the more deliberate lessons she advocates. I feel that explicit focus on the phonological details can be largely avoided. Even native speakers, after all, are rarely conscious of most of these details. On the other hand, Brown is content to help her students with just one colloquial dialect, while I feel that some flexibility in understanding a variety of dialects (though, obviously, not the ability to produce them) is essential, and should be encouraged quite early.

I speak with considerable feeling about the problems of fast speech, because I faced them so severely in Sweden. It was relatively easy for me to gain access to formal varieties of Swedish. I learned to read, to understand the news on the radio, and even to understand the relatively formal language of a classroom lecture, but I was often baffled by the language spoken over coffee cups. It was even difficult for Swedes to tell me how they used their language at this level, for it is, by nature, totally uncodified, and no books or other teaching materials were available that could help me. I found it hard to learn to understand the words and phrases that people used orally but not in writing, and I found it especially hard to learn to recognize the phonologically degenerate remnants of words that I could easily rcognize both in writing and in formal and careful speech.

I refuse to believe that the colloquial style is inherently more complex than more formal styles. On the contrary, I presume that the colloquial is relatively stereotyped with a somewhat restricted vocabulary and possibly even a restricted syntax. This ought to make this style relatively easy to learn if only learners could get access to it and have some means of gaining an understanding of it. Foreigners do not, it should be noted, need to produce this style, at least not during the early stages of learning. They can make themselves understood quite adequately with a fuller and more formal style, but until they can understand the informal style, they will be cut off from informal conversations and from the opportunities for practice that these conversations provide. I see no reason, therefore, to struggle to teach the active use of this style, and I doubt that we could do so very effectively even if we tried. Active use can come only through participaton in real conversations and a long period of immersion. Nevertheless, learners could begin to immerse themselves far more quickly if given some help with comprehension. They cannot use the formal language to answer back if they do not first understand the colloquial language that they hear.

One might suppose that radio and television would offer a rich source of material for practice in understanding the colloquial style. Listening to the radio, or watching television, however, is by no means an efficient way to learn. One can gain some additional practice with the parts of the language that one already understands, but broadcasts give no easy way to extend one's understanding into new areas. In conversation one can ask for explanations for unknown or misunderstood words and expressions, and when reading one can use a dicitonary, but the aural equivalent of a dictionary does not exist. When unknown words or unknown expressions flash by on the radio or television, or even when a phonologically degenerate form of a well-known word flashes by, it disappears before the listener has a chance to find out its meaning. It is difficult to isolate the parts that need learning, or to find any means to learn them. The listener ends up very little wiser than before.

It is for similar reasons that children, like adults, learn much more effectively from language that is directed specifically toward them than from language that is simply present in their surroundings (Ervin-Tripp, 1971; Krashen, 1976). Children do not need to pay attention to language that is not directed toward them, they do not need to understand it, and they have no easy way to expand their understanding of difficult portions. The speaker is not called upon to be careful, to explain, or to repeat. Listen, on the other hand, to any fifteen-minute conversation between close friends or family members. Notice how often somebody asks "What?" or by some other means asks for clarification. Colloquial conversation teeters constantly on the brink of unintelligibility and it is only prevented from toppling over by regular demands for repetition. By making frequent use of requests for repetition and clarification, children learn the meaning of unknown expressions or too rapid bits of speech. Their comprehension progressively expands. If comprehension is to improve, the meanings of things that were not understood before must become clear. Broadcasts and ambient conversations that offer the listener no way of finding out the meaning of unknown parts do not provide an efficient way to learn. Neither do simple tape recordings.

I believe, nevertheless, that my progress in Swedish could have been much faster if I had had many hours of recordings of rapid colloquial conversation together with help in learning to understand them. (See Stanley, 1978, who advocates practice with tapes of the most elliptical styles.) A teacher can guide students through a tape and help them to understand, but other ways of helping learners would be less costly in teacher time and quite possibly less embarrassing or tedious for the student. In particular, written transcripts of recorded conversations would help learners to relate the colloquial language they hear to the more formal language of writing that they learn to understand more easily in other ways. Transcripts would also provide the forms that, when necessary, would permit words to be chased down in a dictionary. Carefully prepared materials would be even more useful if they offered translations or definitons of new and less common words and idioms as they appear. Once again, no effort should be spared from saving the students the pain of thumbing through the dictionary. Their goal, of course, must be to understand the recordings directly and without the crutch of a transcript or a translation, but any means that can speed them toward that end should be offered.

The first colloquial conversations offered to students might be carefully, if artificially, composed in order to make them simple enough for the students' level. They could be staged in a way that would make them more easily understandable. Since students will need to understand the real thing, however, there is good reason to move to natural speeds, natural fast phonology, and natural conversational forms as quickly as possible. Students will need to cope with all the hesitations, false starts, interruptions, overlaps, and background noise to which real conversations are subject. I think it would even be useful to include a good deal of conversation among children and between children and adults among the recordings offered to learners. Children, and adults who speak to children, inevitably use colloquial forms that are marked phonologically by vigorous use of fast speech rules, but their vocabulary and sentence structure should be relatively simple and thus relatively easy to understand.

Students could listen to a conversation several times while reading the transcript and referring to explanations of words and expressions, but they would work toward being able to discard the transcript and still understand the spoken conversation. The students' task would hardly differ from their task when working with a written text for which they have a recording, but starting with a recorded conversation would help them become familiar with a form of the language that arises in a very different context from the kind of edited prose we find in books. Rapid colloquial language will be crucial if our students are to claim fluency, but it is a kind of language that can never be acquired from edited texts alone.

Regularized Spelling

Earlier in the century, linguists such as Jespersen (1904), Palmer (1968), and Sweet (1964) were passionate advocates of phonetic spelling in language teaching. Since their time, enthusiasm for doing much of anything about the bizarre conventional spelling of languages like English and French seems to have waned to the point of disappearance, but this has been more the result of changing fashion than of any systematic investigation into how much help or hindrance a modified spelling might bring. Only with languages that do not use the Roman alphabet are special teaching alphabets or transliterations generally used today.

I became sensitized to the help that modified spelling can give when working with Indonesian. Standard Indonesian spelling follows the spoken language so closely that there is no temptation to modify it in any radical way, but the orthography is defective in one minor respect: The letter "e" is used for two different vowels. Often it stands for a midfront vowel similar to the "e" of "bet," but at times it is used for a weak and unstressed "shwa." Students easily hear the difference between the two vowels, and the use of a single letter for the two sounds probably gives little trouble to native speakers who already know the language. Students of Indonesian as a foreign language, however, make a good many pronunciation errors when they encounter "e" in the spelling of a particular word without knowing which of the two vowels it stands for. It helps students considerably to use the "é" for the full vowel and simple "e" for the shwa, a practice that Indonesians occasionally, though not generally, follow themselves. The accent unambiguously distinguishes the two sounds, and students can then easily associate the written and spoken forms of the word. The accent represents a modest, but obviously useful modification of the standard spelling system. It is easy to use in early lessons, and it is easy to discard later.

Anyone who is willing to grant that the accent is more helpful than distracting for beginning students of Indonesian ought to agree that similar modifications would be desirable for other languages, and yet we seem to be far less comfortable about spelling modifications for more familiar languages such as French or English. Perhaps it is our unfamiliarity with Indonesian, and our lack of any sense of Indonesian "correctness," that makes spelling adjustments seem plausible, but this is hardly an adequate reason to deny beginning students similar help with more familiar languages. Or perhaps this very modest modification for Indonesian seems more acceptable than the more violent adjustments that are needed for languages with less reasonable spelling systems, although it would seem to be precisely where the spelling system is most erratic that help is most needed.

There can be only two objections to the use of a modified spelling system for beginning students: (1) that it looks weird to those accustomed to the conventional spelling, and (2) that the transition to conventional spelling will eventually raise too many difficulties. The first objection is simply the expression of puristic prejudice. It really matters not at all how strange a spelling system looks to the teacher (or to anyone else) as long as it helps the student. The second objection is more serious.

The transition to conventional spelling will be minimized if the introductory spelling system is as close to the conventional one as is compatible with accurate representation of the pronunciation. (An orthography that reflects many of the patterns of the conventional spelling might also soothe the delicate sensibilities of those who shudder at strange transcriptions.) It is foolish to deviate from the standard spelling simply to conform to some other arbitrary standard like the International Phonetic Alphabet. Nor is there any need to indicate every phonetic twitch of a native speaker. Few students, for instance, are likely to be much helped by the widely offered, and almost as widely ignored, IPA transcription of French that can still be seen alongside the standard spelling in many introductory textbooks. It must be intended to show the student how French is pronounced, but it is doubtful that many students find comfort in such passages as this:

səʀaty bjẽto pʀɛ, ʒã̃? nusɔmzẽvite puʀ sɛtœʀ edmi.
ilɛ pʀɛskə lœr dəpaʀtiʀ. ʒəʃɛʀʃ makʀavat ʀuʒ.
(Harris and Lévêque, 1973:400)

This, as any linguist will immediately recognize, is supposed to represent *"Seras-tu bientôt prêt, Jean? Nous sommes invités pour sept heures et demie. Il est presque l'heure de partir. Je cherche ma cravate rouge."*

For most students, it simply does not seem to be worth the time or effort to master the exotic symbols of this transcription and, if it were used at first as the only writing system, it would, indeed, pose some real difficulties when the time came to shift to the conventional spelling.

But one should not abandon all modified spelling simply because it is possible to invent a foolish system. A less radically revised form of French would be just as useful and far more palatable. Instead of omitting silent letters entirely, their silence could be indicated by an accent. This would have the considerable virtue of stabilizing the spelling of the many French words like *les* whose pronunciations vary with the environment: *les hommes, leš femmes*. There is no persuasive reason for substituting the IPA symbols ʀ, ʒ, ʃ, ɛ, e, y, œ, and u for the entirely reasonable French spellings *r, j, ch, e, é, u, eu,* and *ou*. If nasal vowels have to be indicated by any means other than by the following nasal consonant, some sort of ligature that joins the vowel to the following nasal should make the transition to the conventional spelling quite transparent. Since the purpose of a regularized spelling system in the early stages of language instruction is simply to give highly literate students a means of keeping, on paper, a representation of what they hear, it would not seem to matter if the same sound is occasionally spelled in two different ways, unless the teacher feels an urge to check the students' spelling. French has a number of alternative spellings for the same sounds that could be harmlessly retained: double and single consonants; *qu* and *c; e* and *ė; en* and *in,* etc. Contrasting sounds, on the other hand, should surely always be indicated by distinct symbols. With these conventions, the sentences given above might then take a more plausible form— hardly the conventional spelling, but every bit as useful as IPA for indicating pronunciation, and posing far fewer difficulties in the transition to conventional spelling.

> Sĕraš-tu byẽntoĭ prêť, Jãn? Nouš sommĕs invitêš
> pour sepť ħeurĕš éť dĕmie. Il esť presquə l'ħeurĕ
> də partir. Jə cherchĕ ma cravatĕ roujĕ.

Even this transcription may be a shade more radical than necessary, since *i* and *g* might be harmlessly substituted for *y* and *j* in *bientôt* and *rouge*. The *y,* however, has the advantage of being immediatley unambiguous for English speakers, and the *j* conforms to the more common French spelling. On the other hand, a more accurate representation of the pronunciation would substitute *sommez* for *sommes,* but the "s" spelling of the final "z" sound is so common in French (and in English as well) that it might be worth retaining, at least for English-speaking students. The transcription exploits whatever regularities exist in the conventional French spelling, but it would help beginning students listen to spoken French far more perceptively than if they were confined to conventional French orthography. It should, however, pose few transition problems.

A good deal of artistry is needed to work out the details of introductory transcriptions such as this, but they deserve a fairer trial than anyone has been willing to give them in recent years.

6
Vocabulary

As we come to concentrate on comprehension as the first and most important step in language learning, we must also question the extent of the attention that has been lavished upon phonology and syntax, both in language learning research and in the classroom. Students can learn to understand a language with much less self-conscious knowledge of linguistic structure than we have tried to give them; simply by learning to understand they gain a sense of phonology and syntax that eventually will help them to speak. It is not that we need knowledge of linguistic structure in order to use the language, but rather that we need to learn (to understand) the language in order to gain the necessary (largely unconscious) knowledge of linguistic structure that will then allow us to talk.

At the same time, a concentration on comprehension always directs our attention to meaning and to the vocabulary speakers use to convey meaning. We should exercise our full ingenuity in devising ways of helping students expand their receptive vocabulary just as rapidly as possible.

One obvious step is to encourage students to master the art of what has been called "sensible guessing." The meanings of many words can be inferred from context, and students can even be encouraged to pass over some words without feeling that they have to pin down their meanings precisely, as long as their contribution to the passage is relatively minor. Foreign language students might be shown a passage in their native language from which certain words have been removed, as in a cloze test, so they can realize how many of the blanks can be refilled from the context. They should always try to fill the blanks in their new language in the same way, and resort to the dictionary only when there is no alternative. It also saves considerable anguish if students are warned not to waste energy trying to memorize the meanings of rarer words. Students have no way of knowing which unknown words they encounter in a passage are likely soon to appear again, and their lives would be made easier if we could give them guidance.

Students should be persuaded that meaning grows out of context, and that only experience with a vast range of contexts can set the range of a word's meaning. A dictionary can give students a valuable first approximation, but a single dictionary translation rarely tells students all they will eventually want to know about a word. Students must be content with a partial knowledge of meaning at first, and let fuller knowledge develop slowly.

Learning to understand a word can be a strikingly different experience from memorizing it for production. I became vividly aware of this as I struggled to understand Swedish by simultaneously listening and reading. At every stage of my learning, there were hundreds of words that I knew in part but not fully. Not only were there words I could recognize but not recall, but there were also words I could recognize in clear contexts but not in all contexts. There were, moreover, words for which I learned a general meaning before I learned a more specific meaning. There was a time, for instance, when I could recognize several words that meant such things as "skip," "shuffle," "limp," "stomp," tramp," etc., but I did not yet remember which was which. In many cases the precise meaning of words like these is not terribly important, and a general sense of the passage can be gained if one simply knows that the person has moved along in some manner or other.

During my study words were always moving through a penumbra of half knowledge. About some I had only a vague idea, for others a partial idea, for still others a more exact idea. Full knowledge of even a single word, however, requires long experience with its use in all its ramified connotations. It cannot be mastered without long experience with the language.

When one is pressed to use a language productively, the line between knowing and not knowing a word seems sharper. One either knows it well enough to use it in a sentence—a very high standard indeed—or one does not seem to know it at all. But children learn words gradually, and we all continue to expand the vocabulary of our native language gradually. All of us have half-known words that float at the periphery of our knowledge. We recognize words that we would hardly dare use ourselves. Most of us know that "fetlock" and "bridle" have something to do with horses, for instance, but unless we have a special interest in things equestrian, we are likely to be vague on their precise application. Millions of Americans know that automobiles have parts called "manifolds" and "differentials" without being able to point to them and without knowing why they are there. My acquisition of Swedish vocabulary seemed to follow the path that both children and adults use to expand the vocabulary of their native language. To that extent, it seemed a more natural way to learn than did my previous attempts to gain an early and decisive productive control of words.

We can advise students to guess whenever they can. We can urge them at times to be content with only a partial idea of a word's meaning. We can tell them to postpone learning the rarer words. We can provide texts with the kinds of contexts in which words are easily absorbed. In the end, however, not even the best contextual cues, not even the most intelligent guessing, not even the most subtle guidance about important words, can save the student from the time when vocabulary, finally, simply must be mastered. Those thousands of words have to be learned. This is the most painful part of second language learning. It has been the stepchild of second language pedagogy, but it deserves better.

Content Words and Function Words

We can start to understand where our most difficult problems lie by reviewing the familiar distinction between "content words" and "function words." Some words refer to objects, events, actions, or qualities of the world, and seem to have semantic "content." Other words refer less directly to the world outside of language, but are more intertwined with language's internal grammar. These are "function" words, such as prepositions, conjunctions, and various sorts of particles.

It is more accurate to think of content and function words as lying along a continuum than as falling on one side or the other of a simple dichotomy. At one end of the continuum are concrete nouns that stand for visible objects—the most content-full of all content words. At the opposite end are particles, such as determiners and some prepositions, for which it is difficult to point to any coherent meaning at all outside of language. Pronouns lie over toward the function end, although we can sometimes define a pronoun by careful pointing, a feat that is difficult for determiners or prepositions such as "the," "of," or "for." Many verbs and adjectives are closer to the content end, but the more abstract nouns, verbs, and adjectives as well as adverbs seem to be intermediate. If we were to include affixes in our classification, making it a classification of morphemes rather than of words, most affixes would surely be grouped far toward the function end of the continuum.

As one moves toward the content end, the classes grow larger. Nouns often form the largest class of words, while the determiners, prepositions, and conjunctions always form small classes. Verbs are generally second only to nouns in number, and adjectives, if they form a separate class, are likely to be third. Adverbs, once again, are intermediate.

Function words are few in total number but individually very common. Nouns exist in the thousands but no one of them is terribly frequent. There is thus a close inverse correlation between the size of a class and the frequency of its individual members. The most common English noun listed in the Brown University corpus of about a million words of printed English (Kučera and Francis, 1967) is "man," but it is preceded by eighty other more common words. These include determiners, prepositions, conjunctions, pronouns, and a good many auxiliary verbs. Auxiliaries are relatively "functional," however, and other more "content-full" verbs come later. The first determiner is "the" at position one, the first preposition is "of" at position two, and the first conjunction is "and" at position three. As befits their just slightly more content-oriented usage, pronouns begin with "he" at position ten, and most other pronouns are scattered through the first hundred words. Adverbs begin as position twenty-two with "not," and the unambiguous adjectives with "new" at sixty-four, although the more functional "all" (thirty-seven) and "more" (forty-eight) come earlier. The pattern is clear; function words are relatively few in number, but they are individually far more common than content words.

It is interesting to notice how much less information is carried by the function words than by the content words. It is, to be sure, possible to devise ingenious sentences in which the semantic interpretation hinges on the correct understanding of a determiner or a preposition, but such sentences are not at all characteristic of typical English prose. Most function words simply do not supply very much information. This can easily be demonstrated by a passage from which the words farthest toward the function end of the continuum have been replaced by blanks. It is not difficult for an English speaker to get an idea of what such a passage is about, and it is even possible to fill in a good many blanks, although difficulties pile up when several blanks begin to follow one another:

Nearly every _____ Southeast Asia worries _____ spirits _____ one sort _____ another—spirits _____ live _____ trees, _____ lurk _____ roads, _____ _____ hide _____ streams. _____ _____ streams. _____ _____ spirits _____ usually believed _____ _____ _____ _____ ill will _____ men, ceremonies must _____ designed _____ control _____ _____ _____ drive _____ away _____ _____ assure _____ peace _____ health _____ _____ people. Many _____ _____ people _____ Southeast Asia _____ members _____ _____ more systematic religious tradition, _____ _____ rarely troubled _____ _____ notion _____ _____ belief _____ spirits might conflict _____ _____ faith _____ other religious doctrines. (Burling, 1965:3)

If, instead, we remove the nouns from our passage, the meaning falls apart. The next sample omits twenty-two nouns, less than half as many omissions as the forty-eight prepositions, pronouns, conjunctions, and particles removed earlier, but the meaning has now evaporated. The structure of the sentences is fully intact—more transparent than in the first version of the passage—but the sense is gone. It is the content words, nouns among them, that carry the message of the sentence. If these are not understood, the message will not be understood.

Nearly everyone in Southeast _____ worries about _____ of one sort or another— _____ who live in _____, who lurk on _____, or who hide in _____. Because the _____ are usually believed to have nothing but ill _____ toward _____, _____ must be designed to control them or to drive them away and to assure the _____ and _____ of the _____. Many of the _____ in Southeast _____ are _____ of some more systematic religious _____, but they are rarely troubled by the _____ that their _____ in _____ might conflict with their _____ in other religious _____.

The bearing of all this on language learning becomes clear as soon as we note that words near the content end of the continuum tend to be relatively easy to learn. Words for "pictureable" objects, those farthest at the content extreme, seem particularly easy to remember. Words like "tree," "eye," "house," and "woman" cause students of foreign languages very few problems even though there are a great many such words and even though they are not among the most common words in the language. It is even possible to learn content words from a dictionary or by a simple translation. If I tell you that *flicka* means "girl" in Swedish, it is quite possible that twenty-four hours from now you will remember that fact even without special effort. Somehow you can associate the word with an image of the thing it stands for.

Function words pose more difficulties. It is almost impossible to learn the meaning of an extreme function word from a dictionary. Consider the meaning of *de* as given in the glossary of a book edited for French students: "of; with; about, because of; for; from" (Storer, 1952). This list of equivalents merely scratches the surface, but it has surely scratched too deeply to be of much practical help to novices. They would do better simply to infer the meaning of *de* from the context. In fact, as suggested by the first passage given above, the meaning of function words, like *de*, can largely be derived from the linguistic context. *De* has little meaning *except* for contextual meaning; it hardly refers to anything outside of language. This means that there is little need to teach it, just as there is little possibility for teaching its meaning except within its linguistic context. Since the meanings of function words tend to be eccentric and poorly matched from one language to another, it is very difficult to teach them by translation.

The moral is clear: Teach the student enough content words to provide a good context; or, as in the French materials described in Chapter 3, use words from the student's native language to provide the context, and let the use of the function words be inferred from their association with those content words. The function words will gradually be consolidated in the student's memory through repeated and varied exposure in reading and listening. This, of course, is the way the function words are learned in the French reading materials, and it is the way children learn them. Since the function words tend to be very common, they will appear repeatedly, and their use will soon come to seem natural—to "sound right." Getting a feeling for the function words also implies getting a feeling for the grammar, since the grammatical peculiarities of a language manifest themselves predominantly through the function words and through the functional morphemes that we write as affixes. If students are allowed to absorb the use of function words and affixes slowly through long and varied exposure, they can direct their major conscious attention to the area of the language that native and naive speakers also have a self-conscious awareness of—the content words. Although not so difficult individually as the function words, there are so many of them that they will provide plenty of scope for the most energetic student.

Not all content words, of course, are equally easy to learn. Students commonly find the verbs and certain related abstract nouns and adjectives to be the hardest words of all. Verbs are not so easily "pictureable" as nouns. They are not quite so close to the content end of the continuum. They far outnumber the proper function words, however, and individually they are less common, so students get less insistent exposure to them than to the individual prepositions and conjunctions. Similarly, abstract nouns—"disappointment," "pride," "request"—are always more difficult to remember than more concrete nouns—"blouse," "nose," "carrot." If I tell you that *beroende* means "dependence" in Swedish, the chances are good that you will forget it before you forget the meaning of *flicka*.

The schematic diagram in Figure 4 is intended to summarize the relationships among various classes of words. The dots on the chart represent the concentration of words of various classes and at various frequencies. Thus, the function words, the most common words in a language, are densely clustered at the bottom. Concrete content words are individually less common, but they extend in large numbers up and off the top of the chart. Between these extremes is a thick cloud of abstract verbs, adjectives, and nouns.

Four regions are distinguished on the chart, and, while the boundaries are somewhat arbitrary, they indicate areas of vocabulary that pose different sorts of problems for learners. The words of Section A cause massive difficulties during the early stages of traditional language courses where production is emphasized, but they cause much less difficulty in a course that focuses on comprehension, since they carry so little referential meaning. With adequate passive experience, they can become natural rather quickly and easily, since they are high in frequency and relatively few in number. The words in Section C cause relatively few problems, but for a different reason—being highly concrete they are easy to remember in spite of their large number and individual rarity.

Section D contains the less common and less essential words of the language. This section continues indefinitely upward, for there is no end to a language's stock of words. No one can ever master them all and, in early language instruction, we can hardly worry about this less common and more specialized vocabulary.

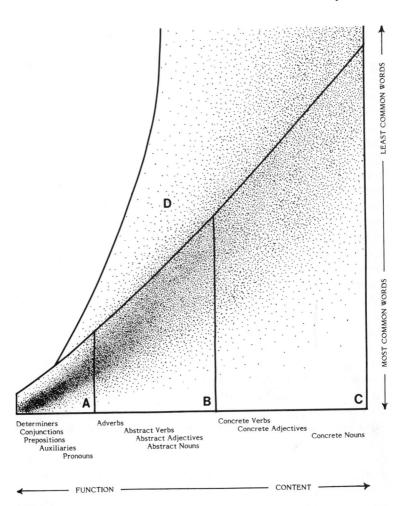

Determiners
Conjunctions
Prepositions
Auxiliaries
Pronouns

Adverbs
Abstract Verbs
Abstract Adjectives
Abstract Nouns

Concrete Verbs
Concrete Adjectives
Concrete Nouns

FUNCTION   CONTENT

Figure 4

Having learned the vocabulary of Sections A, B, and C, students must move out on their own and continue to expand their vocabulary in whatever direction their interests take them.

This leaves Section B, and it is these words that cause the most problems. They carry sufficient content to be needed for proper understanding, but they are too abstract to be easily remembered. They exist in too great a number, but each one occurs too infrequently to be as readily absorbed as the high frequency but less numerous function words. The single area of language where

students need the most help is in building up their comprehension of abstract nouns, verbs, adjectives, and adverbs. Students of foreign languages have always known that this is where
the difficulties lie. It seems to have been less obvious to their
teachers.

Graded Readers

Once we resolutely focus on vocabulary recognition as the central
problem of language learning, it becomes a terrible temptation to
design graded materials where vocabulary can be systematically
introduced and where each new word can be repeated often
enough and reviewed regularly enough to ensure retention by the
student. Carefully graded readers and graded recordings look like
the obvious way to skirt the major difficulty students have with
unprepared texts: the vast number of unfamiliar words, and their
ignorance about which words deserve to be learned first. All too
often, students struggle valiantly to memorize a word that will not
appear again for another five hundred pages.

But specially prepared texts also have a terrible drawback.
Only a genius like Dr. Seuss can control vocabulary and still write
a book that is fun to read. Few of us who try to prepare teaching
materials in foreign languages can claim the skill of a Dr. Seuss.
We can never succeed in producing as interesting a narrative as
can a good original writer. Any difficulties caused by the uncontrolled vocabulary of natural prose strike me as being more than
offset by the interest that a skilled writer can bring to her
work. This does not mean that one should exercise no judgment.
If I were teaching English, I would certainly choose Hemingway
over Joyce, and I might even consider *Winnie the Pooh* or *Alice in
Wonderland* if their sentence structure and vocabulary proved to
offer a relatively easy starting point. But until textbook writers rise
to the level of A.A. Milne or Lewis Carroll, we will do better to stick
to interesting original writing. The appeal of a good story will
make up for almost any eccentricity in vocabulary.

There are, moreover, obvious ways—short of resorting to texts
with artificially restricted vocabulary—by which lesson designers
and teachers can help beginning students through a text with a
rich vocabulary. The most obvious is to translate the rarer words
within the text so that the students' reading need not be

interrupted, even by a search among the footnotes. This would make reading more fun and simultaneously let the students know that they should not bother trying to remember some of the new words quite yet.

Building Vocabulary

One way to help students gain receptive control over the difficult type "B" vocabulary—the mass of abstract verbs, nouns, and adjectives of intermediate frequency—is to gather related words together into sets so that the associations among them can be seen, and so that they can give each other mutual support. Consider, for instance, these lists of Swedish words:

ro	rest, repose
roa	amuse, entertain
rolig	amusing, funny
oro	agitation, disturbance, anxiety
oroa	disturb, harass
orolig	anxious, uneasy
del	part
delning	division
deltaga	to take part
deltagare	participant
delägare	partner
delvis	partly
avdelning	part, division
andel	share
fördel	advantage
fördelaktig	advantageous
nackdel	disadvantage
odelad	undivided, whole
tredjedel	one third
fjärdedel	one fourth

These words obviously form families built around the roots *ro* and *del*. Most of the prefixes and suffixes that decorate the roots occur in many other words, and one needs no vast experience reading and listening before these affixes become familiar enough to give plausibility to their combinations with the roots. Nevertheless, knowing the root and the affix is not enough to confidently predict the meaning of the derived term. The situation is precisely the same as in English where "part," "partner," and "participant" are obviously related but where a knowledge of "part," "-ner" and "-icipant" would not be enough, by itself, to tell a novice the meaning of the derived words. The student must eventually learn each of the words derived from *ro* and *del* individually, but the task can be made easier if the relationships among them are recognized. No one of these words is terribly common. They are among that great middle mass of type "B" terms that must be known before easy reading or aural comprehension can be claimed, but that are neither common enough to ensure ample exposure nor concrete enough to be easily visualized. Students might read and listen for a long time before encountering some of these words, but collectively they are by no means rare. One or another of them turns up with regularity.

Enterprising students will notice some of these relationships as they thumb through the dictionary, although the arrangement of our dictionaries makes it easier to notice related words with different suffixes than those with different prefixes. Even when the relationships are noticed, however, it is difficult for students to use their observations systematically. They have no way to know which of the related words they see are worth taking note of and which are too rare to be worth the trouble. Words in a dictionary moreover, lack context; this makes them far less appealing and less easy to remember than words encountered in reading and listening.

When preparing materials for student use, it should not be difficult to isolate the word families that are well-represented in a particular passage, and point them out to the students. This would allow them to take special note of these sets of related words and encourage them to make a special effort to remember them as they appear in context. Instead of coping with several individually rare words, they would then have a chance to learn a single family, representatives of which crop up with considerable frequency. Each occurrence of any single word might help them all to become solidified in memory.

A parallel possibility is to gather together words that are confusingly similar in sound or spelling, even though unrelated in meaning. By bringing groups of words together, such as the following list from Swedish, specific differences can be noticed, and perhaps they will be remembered more clearly when next encountered in context.

skild	separate, different
skuld	guilt, debt
skull	[for the] sake [of]
skyla	to cover
skylla	blame
skylt	sign [board]

It is less easy to collect lists of misleadingly similar words than of genuinely related words, however, and it is probably less useful. Since different students will surely confuse different sets, it is hard to guess which confusions will need sorting out; however, help might be offered for the points of confusion that are most typical. Once again, it would seem best to confine such study to words that actually occur in the texts under study, for we must never forget that vocabulary needs a full context to give it substance. All other devices for teaching vocabulary are merely aids to the use of the full texts, spoken and written.

For languages that share many words with English, especially the Germanic and Romance languages, it is also useful to point out the most common sound and letter correspondences. A modest understanding of the sound changes that have separated German from English can help an English speaker make sensible guesses about the meanings of a great many German words. A similar understanding of the equivalents between English and French spelling conventions can help a student recognize and remember French words.

There is one type of word list that is *not* likely to be of much use to receptive learners—a list of words with related meanings. Such a list can be useful for learners who want to speak (see the section below on production). They may wish to express a particular time and, having studied a list of time expressions they may search their memory and come up with the right choice. But readers and listeners cannot know the semantic domain of the next word they will face. They must start from the form of that word and use that form while searching in memory. What receptive learners need, therefore, are memory techniques that are based on, and that start from the form of words, rather than the meaning of words.

The Key-Word Method

Mnemonics, the science or art of memory, has been given little attention in modern Western education. We want our students to understand principles and patterns, not to memorize facts. We have not offered our students much help in dealing with the areas of language learning that call for simple memory, possibly because to do so would seem to violate our belief that sheer memorization is an undesirable component of education. To learn a language, however, demands memory of a large number of highly arbitrary facts, and if mnemonic aids are useful anywhere, then language learning, and in particular vocabulary learning, should be the place.

Language learners apparently differ considerably in the strategies by which they memorize. Some, more or less self-consciously, try to learn words as part of longer phrases, proverbs, or poems. Some search quite deliberately for mental associations that will bind the new word to something they already know. Some try, by brute force, to memorize long lists or thick bundles of flash cards. Some hardly bother, and simply wait for words to be learned "naturally." It may well be that an important difference between those students who learn language quickly and those who do not lies quite simply in the superior strategies by which the faster learners memorize. Language researchers have paid little attention to these strategies and have offered little help to struggling students, probably because of the devaluation of mere memory in our educational system. Nevertheless, any kind of trick that helps students fix words in memory and thereby speeds up the process of language learning deserves to be explored.

One mnemonic trick that has received a good deal of attention in the last few years has been named the "key-word" method. To anyone who abhors the idea of memorizing isolated words, and to anyone who disapproves of relying on the native language when learning a new language, the key-word methods may seem absurd, but the reported results are so striking that we have to pay attention (Ott et al., 1973; Atkinson, 1975; Levin, 1979; Merry, 1980).

When trying to learn the meaning of a foreign term, students are advised to think of some word in their own language that sounds or looks like all or part of the foreign word. This is the "key word." For instance, in trying to learn the Swedish word *brits*, "bunk," I thought of the slang term *Brit* meaning someone from

Great Britain. Next, the student is supposed to construct some association, however bizarre, that connects the meaning of the foreign term to the meaning of the key word. I conjured up a vision of the British Isles coverd with bunk beds and filled with *Brits*. The next time I encounter the word *brits* I am supposed to think: *Brits*—that sounds like *Brit;* oh yes, I see a picture in my mind of a lot of Britishers lying in their bunks. *Ergo: brits* must mean "bunk."

The system seems foolishly roundabout. We want our students to form direct associations between the new words and their concepts. We would even like them to leave their native language out of it altogether. Here is a method that not only makes use of the native language, but also makes use of a word that has nothing to do with the meaning one is looking for, and it proposes an apparently tortuous chain of associations. Nevertheless, those who have experimented with the key word method report a 50 percent increase in the rate of vocabulary retention. Why should such a system work?

Perhaps it works simply because it draws attention to vocabulary and makes students concentrate on vocabulary in an organized way. It is a method that lies between the brutal but direct struggle with word lists or flash cards and the touching hope that, if learners simply let the language wash over them by reading and listening, they will eventually absorb everything without much concerted effort. The key-word method focuses attention on vocabulary without pushing learners to the mindlessness of a word list or a set of flash cards.

Of course, if students fail to outgrow their key words the system is hopeless. I have a vision of a student progressing slowly through a text; groping, with each word, for some strange key word and the image this key word evokes; or stopping a conversation in order to construct a bizarre image. This, of course, is hardly what is intended, and if the method is to work at all, students must gradually outgrow the key words and gradually form a direct connection between their new word and its meaning. But the method should not be rejected out of hand, and teachers ought to try it themselves. When I first tried it, my reaction was mild annoyance that such a foolish method seemed to work. It allowed me, with unreasonable ease, to remember the meaning of *brits*, and possibly the reader will have inadvertently learned its meaning too. As I tried the method on more words, I became increasingly annoyed at myself for not having been smart enough to think of the method myself, and annoyed at all my language teachers for never letting me in on the secret. We should inquire more carefully into methods that effective learners use and then share their secrets. Perhaps several other clever mnemonic tricks are out there waiting to join the key-word method.

The key-word method, however, shares with all other methods that focus on vocabulary the danger that it will convey to students the idea that language consists simply of an unordered heap of words, and that simply by memorizing words with sufficient diligence one can learn a language. I believe we have paid too little attention to ways of building up vocabulary, but I would not want to push too hard in the other direction. In the end, all aids to vocabulary learning ought to be kept within bounds, for words, finally, belong in a context. They need to be surrounded by other words, and the subtleties of their meanings will only emerge as they are repeatedly encountered in a variety of contexts. It is easier, more fun, and more useful to study sentences than to study isolated words, and even better than isolated sentences are connected texts, written or spoken. Most of a student's time and effort should surely be spent with passages that are long enough to provide a full context, both linguistic and semantic, for the individual words. It is in such contexts that new words will most readily be consolidated in memory; moreover, it is by means of such passages that the student will get the best possible sense of how the language works.

Production

The thesis of this book is that the greatest emphasis in formal language instruction should be given to comprehension. I know of no persuasive evidence that learning to *speak* plays any significant role whatsoever in learning to understand. Indeed, I am confident that it is entirely possible to gain a native-like ability to understand a language without any serious effort at speaking. On the other hand, there is no way by which a person can become a fluent speaker unless he can understand. Speaking is so dependent on comprehension that it has to be seen as the derivative, secondary skill.

Nevertheless, a comprehension ability alone will hardly satisfy most students, and language teachers certainly have an obligation to prepare their students for speaking. Their first contribution to this end is probably to persuade the students to be patient, and to encourage them to wait until they can understand a good deal and until they feel comfortable about the language before trying to say much of anything. Still, the time will eventually come when students will want to talk. How do we help them?

The most important thing to remember is that speaking, when it finally comes, should grow out of a large fund of accumulated knowledge. Students should not need instruction in new facts but simply encouragement about activating their receptive knowledge. It would be pleasant to imagine that, once students hear enough of the language, it would be impossible to stop them from talking—just as it is impossible to stop two-year-old children from talking—but adults are often impatient and some systematic encouragement is likely to be helpful.

In the long run there is only one way to achieve fluency: go where the language is spoken and chatter with the natives. However, there may be some value in preparing students for the first few days and weeks after they step off the plane. Perhaps we can clarify our challenge, and theirs, by recognizing that, when the crunch finally comes and when a learner really wants to talk, some things are important immediately. Others can be postponed.

What the new learner will *not* need is impeccable grammar. Anyone who waits for impeccable grammar before being willing to speak will wait a very long time. Better an easy willingness to get along as best as one can. Schumann and others have noted the similarities of a stage of second language acquisition to pidginization (Schumann, 1978a, 1978b; Andersen, 1979), and if we are realistic, we will be happy when our students construct their own rough and ready pidgins in an effort to get their meaning across, and we will not let them be disappointed when, in the heat of real conversation, they are unable to construct perfect sentences. Anyone can invent a pidgin if pushed into an extreme situation, so we hardly have to teach the skill; but we might, at least, encourage our students to feel that this is a legitimate and appropriate first step on the way to speaking a language. A pidgin allows one to try out one's wings. It is the adult equivalent of the stage of baby talk that everyone must pass through when learning one's first language. What does a learner's pidgin amount to?

What anyone does, who is pushed by the brutal necessity of communication in a language he controls poorly, is to strip away most of the inflections and resort to short sentences and straightforward word order. Grammar can be sacrificed and pronunciation may be haphazard, but what speakers cannot do without are words. This is always the aspect of language that is most readily manipulable by a speaker, and new learners always direct most of their conscious effort to the search for words. Words are even used where a native speaker might use grammatical markers. Adverbs substitute for tenses, and numbers or words such as "many" replace plurals. This is not a subtle form of communication, and every learner will want to move beyond it, but it amounts to a realistic first step.

By accepting the inevitability of pidginization during early attempts to speak, learners are free to focus on vocabulary, and if they can pull out enough words they will be able to start. If they have heard and understood enough of the language, the words will soon begin to fit together into patterns that sound right to the natives; then the learners will begin to outgrow their pidgin, but this is impossible in the beginning.

Not all words are equally important, however, nor are all words equally difficult. On first arriving in a foreign country a visitor hardly needs an active abstract vocabulary of literature, economics, or philosophy. This can wait. On the other hand, names for concrete objects, such as the names of the local foods (to say nothing of names of local cities, streets, and people, which we do not usually think of as part of the language but which must be learned along with the names of all the other local objects), are learned so easily once one is on the ground that little is gained by expending great effort on them ahead of time. But other, more functional parts of the vocabulary are needed very early and, if we can learn what these most necessary words are, we should be able to offer specific help to our students.

A proposal that strikes me as offering considerable promise for helping students when they begin to talk is the "Notional Syllabus" of D.A. Wilkins (1972a, 1976). Wilkins wants to emphasize the content of the communication (*what* we want to speak about) rather than the structure of the language (*how* we speak). Instead of grammatical categories, he proposes that we should organize our courses around such categories as time, quantity, location, agent, instrument, and degree of certainty. These are semantic categories, though not the kinds of categories we find in common phrase books ("food and restaurants," "car and travel," "clothing," etc.). Rather, they are the categories of meaning that need to be expressed whatever the topic of our conversation. Whatever a person wants to talk about, he will need the notional categories that Wilkins asks us to emphasize.

My own experience in Sweden confirmed very strongly for me the need for control of the areas that Wilkins stresses, and I would modify his proposal only to the extent of suggesting that we can operationalize his categories and make them easier to introduce by concentrating on the words by which their meanings are expressed. During my first weeks in Sweden, I easily soaked up scores of names for concrete objects. These came so easily that I felt that any deliberate effort to learn them ahead of time would have been misplaced. Once those Swedish objects were there to be seen and touched, their labels came easily. At the same time, I found myself struggling very hard for control of several kinds of more abstract terms. I urgently needed these to express myself, and I even felt that I would have wanted terms for the same ideas whatever language I had been working on. On the basis of my experience in Sweden, I suggest that prospective travelers could be prepared by helping them learn to use words in several specific categories (Burling, 1980). As always, of course, I am assuming that students will already "know" these words, and that their task is now to learn to produce them quickly and fluently on the right occasion.

1. *Greetings and courtesy phrases.* The local equivalents of "hello," "goodby," "thank you," etc., are needed from the first day. Without them a person is mute; with them, she begins to be a social being.

2. *Language.* This is such a salient concern that it becomes a constant topic of conversation. A few basic words and expressions for language will be useful at once: "word," "talk," "say," "understand," "translate," etc.

3. *Quantity.* Numbers and a few related words, "many," "times," "a little," "more," etc., are also needed very early, at least in any modern commercial and industrial society. Prices, time, distance, and age all require numbers.

4. *Money and shopping.* A new arrival must soon be able to name the units of currency and use such words as "price," "buy," "sell," etc.

5. *Modals.* The ideas expressed by modals—"can," "should," "may," "must," etc.—are needed by anyone who is groping about in unfamiliar circumstances and who hopes to be reasonably polite. In many languages, of course, these ideas are expressed through very different devices than the modals of English, but in one way or another the ideas must be expressed.

6. *Pronouns.* These are needed as soon as one tries to pass beyond the communicative stage of brute pointing.

7. *Questions and answers.* So many of the earliest experiences of communication involve questions and answers that the learner should quickly learn to ask "where?" "when?" "why?" etc., and to answer "yes," "no," "maybe," and "I don't know."

8. *Conjunctions and subordinators.* An adult is not long content with simple sentences. Adults need to be able to say "and," "or," "but" and "if," and very soon want to attempt relative and subordinate clauses. The simplest (but only the simplest) devices for building up complexity deserve early attention.

9. *Indefinites.* Without equivalents for "somebody," "nowhere," "anything," etc., learners will soon find themselves in hopeless corners.

10. *Time.* Languages use a wide variety of syntactic and lexical devices for expressing time, and learners soon need some means for talking about time. A good deal can be accomplished with the names of weekdays and months and with clock time, but before long learners will also need to say "today," "this evening," "hour," "year," "later," "ago," etc.

11. *Space and location.* Space may cause fewer problems than time because one can gesture and point, and because the names for streets and cities are relatively easy and offer a simple means for organizing space. Demonstratives and a few prepositions (or equivalent expressions) can be a help, however, and

verbs of motion and position such as "go," "come," "ride," "dwell," "move," "go get," "sit," "put," "open," etc., are needed quite early.

12. *Aspect.* English does not have a grammatical category of "aspect," but speakers need words that convey what "aspect" accomplishes in some languages: "begin," "end," "still," "now and then," "again," "not yet."

13. *Sensory and cognitive terms.* Words for such concepts as "know," "believe," "look at," "hear," "remember," and "forget" are also needed quite early.

14. *Logical and temporal connectives.* There comes a time when learners will no longer be satisfied with "and," "but," "or," and "if," and will feel a need for ways of building up more complex logical and temporal interdependence: "because of," "instead of," "so that," "on account of," "even though," "especially," "before," "any longer," etc.

15. *Probability, source of knowledge and attitude.* As learners gain experience, they will want to qualify what they say with the kind of information that we express in English with "probably," "of course," "really," "possibly," "usually," "unfortunately," "hope," "want," "apparently," "he said," etc.

These fifteen groups of words are not grammatical categories (although these ideas are expressed through grammatical categories in some languages) nor are they the traditional semantic categories of phrase books. They are closer to the notional categories of Wilkins, and they represent areas that can easily cause difficulty for one who is just starting to use the language. They are the areas that a new speaker needs in order to achieve a minimal level of expressive ability. If students are to be given any help with production, it is probably areas such as these that deserve the most emphasis.

Of course the fifteen groups of words give only a framework for supporting the particular topic that one wants to talk about. A speaker also must be interested in, and have the words for, the topics. It is only while attempting to express oneself on topics of interest that a learner will need these categories or gain practice in using them.

Students are not likely to gain real fluency with these categories, or with any others, until they finally go traveling, and all we can hope to do is give them a bit of a head start for that time. As long as we are confined to a classroom, I know of no better way of starting than to follow Leonard Newmark's suggestion for a "Minimal Language-Teaching Program" (Newmark, 1971). A fluent speaker, ideally a native, engages the students in conversation, and they do their best to get their meaning across. The goal is the exchange of information, and the means are whatever resources the student can call upon. Newmark's goal is to get people to converse on subjects that are of genuine interest, and he cares little about correctness or about sequencing of difficulty. The method comes as close to mimicking real conversation as is possible within the four walls of a classroom.

If the experience of talking is to be realistic, it must have communication as its central goal. Reciting drills and repeating formulas is of little profit, but role playing and staging impromptu conversations in which students try to achieve pragmatic ends can be useful and fun. As always, there is the danger that students will learn too much from one another, but this danger will be minimized if they have already heard, and learned to understand, massive amounts of the language as spoken by a native speaker. This ought to provide a firm point of reference, and allow students to monitor their own speech and gradually correct their own errors. Free, relatively undirected and uncriticized exchange of information is probably the best way to encourage productivity in our students.

What we must finally do, however, if we really expect our students to talk, is to send them somewhere where they can talk. Only then can they finally activate their language in a realistic context. If we can teach them (to understand) the language first, then the final step of activating their passive knowledge should take place with some efficiency.

An Integrated Course

The techniques that I have proposed should support each other, and they should provide enough variety to hold a learner's interest. We ought to think more often, however, about the most useful speed and intensity with which to pursue language instruction.

Peter Strevens (1977:28ff.; see also Deveny and Bookout, 1976) has made the plausible claim that the more hours spent studying a language each day, the more will be learned each hour. In other words, a person who studies a language for eight hours every day for one week can expect to learn more than by spending just one hour each day for a period of eight weeks. Perhaps language is so easily forgotten that gaps of even a few hours reduce the overall efficiency of learning. If this is true, then typical American high schools and colleges, where students take four or five courses simultaneously and where the study of a foreign language is spread out over several years, provide a dismally inefficient schedule for language study. It might be far better to work on a language full time for a relatively brief period. After a half term at full time, students should be able to get further with a language than after a full year at quarter time. If that half term could be devoted primarily to the comprehension half of the language, and if the production half were postponed, a very modest goal would be to reach the present second year level in reading and in aural comprehension after a half term. Most students ought to be able to do much better.

After a lively session with a monolingual demonstration, I envisage students spending several hours each day listening to the language. They could listen to many kinds of texts, long and short, colloquial and formal, recorded and live, but always under conditions where they would have to attend to the meaning. They could demonstrate their understanding in various ways—by pressing a button, by physical action, or by checking a box on a piece of paper—but they would not be required to say anything themselves. I think that written transcripts of some of the things they hear would help them make more rapid and satisfying progress.

At the same time, I would have students work with written texts. I believe the advantages of adult materials that have intrinsic interest for adult students are so overwhelming that it is better to prepare adult texts with native language supports than to use childish texts that need less support. The quickest way I know to work students into comfortable use of adult level foreign texts is by means of mixed materials such as I describe in Chapter 3.

Students who worked no more than one quarter time with my French materials reached the point, after about eight weeks, where they could read unmixed adult materials, although their reading rate remained slow and they preferred texts that had been prepared with footnotes and a glossary. In a full-time course in a Western European language, English-speaking students should easily be able to achieve the same level in no more than three weeks, even while spending much of their time on more colloquial and less literary oral comprehension. As soon as the texts reach the point where the majority of the running text is in the foreign language (certainly no later than the second week), it would be worthwhile providing a taped version of the text (perhaps of the full foreign text without English mixture) so that students will be forced to read too rapidly to translate everything. This way they will avoid spelling pronunciatons, and intonational cues can help them sort through the syntax. Moving rapidly into adult texts would very quickly give students all the grammar they need for comprehension.

As the weeks pass, I would expect grammatical and phonological problems to recede so far into the background that students would feel their greatest and most nagging problem to be that of gaining a receptive command of vocabulary, both for reading and for oral comprehension. I would certainly offer them whatever help is available in the form of cognate and borrowing patterns or mnemonic tricks, but I would always expect vocabulary to be consolidated by encountering the words repeatedly in a wide variety of texts, spoken and written. Providing a large quantity of texts for both listening and reading would be the most essential task of the teacher and the course designer, and as the students listen and read, they would, partially unconsciously, build up a solid sense of both phonology and grammar. Students should be pushed to understand rapid spoken colloquial conversation as well as the more formal varieties of the language, for only in that way will they finally be able to sustain a conversation.

During the final two weeks of a full-time half term of study, it would probably be worthwhile spending an hour or two each day encouraging students to start to talk. By then, many of them surely would be eager to try and they would have acquired the appropriate background. At this point, more would surely be achieved by focusing on the communication of information than by focusing on the niceties of grammar, but some special attention could be given to those categories of meaning that are most essential when one first tries to use a language for practical purposes.

By the end of the half term, I would expect students to be able to read at least as well as our students do when they now finish the second year of their language class, a bit slowly to be sure, and requiring occasional support of a dictionary, but skillfully enough to be useful. With specific attention to oral comprehension I would expect them to be able to understand both the formal and colloquial spoken styles of the language considerably more easily than most students do after two years of study. Their ability to speak could not be expected to match second-year students, but they would have laid a foundation for the rapid development of productive skills once they have the right opportunity.

A program of this sort holds out one additional promise: It might allow students to learn languages where social factors pose special barriers. Language communities differ markedly in their tolerance for broken speech. When a language is regularly learned by foreigners, its speakers may be forced to be relatively tolerant. English is so often learned as a second language that English speakers often have wide experience with foreign accents and uncertain grammar. We make allowances for foreigners, and we expect to use English even with speakers of severely limited abilities. Some other languages, however, particularly those spoken by small numbers of people, are rarely learned as second languages. Few adults ever try to learn an American Indian language, for instance, and those who do, face serious barriers because Indians have no experience in dealing with foreigners who are struggling with their language. Indians know too much English. In encounters between an Indian and an English speaker, English is almost always used, and the habit of using English as the contact language is very difficult to escape. For the non-Indian, it is always awkward to attempt to speak Iroquois or Navajo with someone whose English is so embarrassingly superior to one's own Iroquois or Navajo. From the other side, Indians have little experience with non-Indians trying to learn their languages, and it must be difficult to cope with the odd character who tries.

An initial focus on comprehension would allow a pedagogy for such languages in which a great deal of the language would be learned before any attempt is made to speak it. Only after learning the language would the novice be subjected to the embarrassment of trying to speak, and only then would the native speaker be subjected to the agony of hearing his language distorted. With a sufficient knowledge of the language gained through initial training in comprehension, both the embarrassment and the agony should be much reduced.

A course that emphasizes comprehension, moreover, is especially adaptable to materials that students can use by themselves with relatively little active assistance from a living teacher. If written materials and tapes could be properly organized, well-motivated students should be able to work through them largely on their own. This opens the attractive possibility that even languages of very low demand could become accessible to the occasional student who wants one, and instruction might then become less dependent on assembling a class of ten or more students.

The only reasonable follow-up to an intensive half term such as I have described, or to a period of self-study with comprehension materials from an uncommonly taught language, would be a period of immersion in the proper foreign language setting. A second half term among native speakers of the language should allow the students to activate their passive skills. After one full term devoted to a single goal, they would have spent no more time than they would spend in two full years of a typical foreign language class and, with the steady reduction of travel costs, this should hardly be much more expensive than board, room, and tuition at home.

After their term with the language, students might not know much formal grammar. They might not be able to conjugate a verb or recite the prepositions that take the dative. On the other hand, they would surely be able to understand, read, and speak with more skill and a great deal more confidence than the typical product of our second-year language courses. One suspects that they would also have had far more fun.

Some Implications

One article of the Chomskian faith has been the assertion that the most important, or at least the most interesting, component of language arises from the innate, inherited characteristics of the human mind. It is the innate ability to learn and to use a language that distinguishes us from other animals, and the built-in constraints of our minds are presumed to shape all human languages in similar ways. The features that vary from one language to another must, of course, be learned before one can claim to know a language, but the implication of the Chomskian doctrine is that these are relatively minor and peripheral—or at least they are less interesting than the universal features. With the investigation of the universal features we have the most promising available means to gain insight into the nature of the human mind.

The polemic over innateness, like so many of the polemics that grew up around Chomskian linguistics, has been less illuminating than silly. I doubt if anyone ever denied that certain aspects of language are innate. Nor can it be reasonably doubted that particular languages have to be learned. Instead of engaging in polemics, we should be inquiring into the extent of learning and the extent of innate knowledge. No one should ever have had to stake out an extreme position on one side or the other in futile debate about nature and nurture. When Chomsky first wrote, a modest corrective may have been needed for an earlier disregard of innate knowledge and universals, and Chomsky certainly made that corrective. Now a corrective from the opposite side seems in order, and we ought to consider the learned component of language more seriously.

For it does remain the case that one of the most notable universal features of language is precisely that languages have to be learned. It is not difficult, after all, to imagine a language with the same degree of complexity as a human language, but that is fully determined by the genetic endowment of the organism. In some ways, of course, such a language would be very different from the human languages we know. It would be invariable, except as individuals vary in their hereditary makeup; it would not change through time except as the slow pressures of natural selection gradually alter the species; it would not have to be learned.

The communication systems of the social insects, though quite complex, are presumably of this sort. They seem to be utterly fixed by the animal's inheritance, they require no learning, and they cannot be changed. We know of no limits on inherited complexity that would make an inherited language of the human degree of complexity impossible, but our languages are not of this sort. How, then, has it happened that we, unlike the social insects, have evolved a communication system that requires such an enormous investment of learning?

The Hardware and Software of Language

One way to think about this question is by an analogy with the distinction made by computer specialists between hardware and software. Hardware is fixed. It is the basic machinery. Software is the program that is used to instruct the machinery, and it is changeable, flexible, fluid. By altering the software, the programmer can make the same piece of hardware do quite different things. The designer of the equipment has considerable choice about how much to build into his hardware, and how much to leave for programming in software. The designer can, in other words, choose to build into the hardware the capacity to be flexibly programmed by software. A specialized machine, designed for a narrow purpose, may be more efficient if its purposes are firmly and rigidly embedded in its hardware. A machine destined for many purposes, even for purposes not originally foreseen by its designers, is better if it is sufficiently flexible to be adapted to a wide range of uses by an equally wide range of software.

We can compare the innate and the learned components of language to the hardware and software components of a computer. The innate component of language is hardwired into us. It is this inherited hardware that is the basis for the universal aspects of language. The learned component of language must be programmed into us, just as the software component must be programmed into a computer.

By comparison with other animals, human beings can be programmed with a vast and intricate software. This, to be sure, is only a jargony way of saying that learning is more important for humans than for other animals. Still, it calls attention to the rather special and remarkable direction that evolution took when the human line began to branch away from the other primates. Our early ancestors acquired, above all, the ability to be variously and flexibly programmed for a wide range of behavior. Among other things, we can be variously programmed to understand and to speak different languages.

In the course of human evolution, new hardware developed that now provides us with our basic inherited capacity for language. This, as much as any other characteristic, distinguishes us from our nonspeaking primate cousins. One of the most basic hardware changes supporting this distinction is our vastly expanded capacity to accept and store a program. Our hardware is designed like that of a flexible computer. Far more can be added to our minds through learning than can be added to the mind of any other animal.

It seems obvious that evolution could proceed more quickly through an expansion of the brain's storage capacity, and the corresponding expansion of its ability to receive and store programs, than through other more specific and delicate reorganization of its hardware. Every hardware change has to arise through mutation, then pass through long generations of testing by natural selection, before it is finally built reliably into the chromosomes. No doubt this process has brought important and subtle changes to our hardware; but, of all the conceivable changes, the one that would produce the most dramatic payoff, from a relatively modest physical change, would be the expansion of storage capacity. This implies a shift to a greater reliance on learning as a governor of behavior and a correspondingly reduced reliance on inflexible heredity. The increased reliance on learning was already evident in primates, as compared with other mammals, and in all mammals as compared with other vertebrates, but the trend has extended much further with humans. This, to be sure, greatly increases the time and effort each individual needs to get programmed, and this is why human maturation is such a long slow process. In some ways we are a less efficient species than we would be if our knowledge and behavior were more fully hardwired in by heredity, but we are also a far more adaptable species. It is the potential for being variously programmed that provides the basis for all kinds of cultural variability, including, in particular, linguistic variability. To ask what aspects of our language are hardwired into our brains, ears, and vocal organs, and to contrast these aspects with those other aspects that require programming, is merely another way of asking which aspects are innate and which are learned. However, understanding the relative evolutionary ease of multiplying storage capacity, compared to other kinds of hardware changes, may help us understand why the balance has tipped so far toward learning. We have acquired both an unprecedented need and an unprecedented ability to learn, but this could have evolved through a relatively simple expansion of the kinds of storage capacity already possessed in more limited degree by other primates.

Of course, I would not deny that we have also acquired, in the course of our evolution, a great deal of more specific, inherited, linguistic hardwiring. Certainly, for instance, we have an innate ability to distinguish the noises of language from other noises, to know that language noises can refer to things, and to know that these noises can be put into orderly arrangements. I also find it entirely plausible to suppose that we also have hardwired into us many of the more specific bits of syntactic knowledge that Chomsky and others have pointed to as evidence of our innate capacity for language. Even some aspects of our lexical abilities are surely inherited, such as our capacity to recognize certain phenomena as plausibly nameable. As Berlin and Kay (1969) have demonstrated so convincingly, for instance, certain colors are more readily nameable than others, and it must be our innate perceptual abilities that are responsible for the salience of these colors (Kay and McDaniel, 1978). Since our perceptual abilities reach back even beyond the time when distinctively human language began to develop, our language must depend in part upon innate propensities that were not, at least in origin, specifically linguistic.

While acknowledging that language rests firmly on inherited capacity, we should not be dazzled by the brilliance of Chomsky's rhetoric into forgetting that there is also much in language that is variable and that has to be learned. Individuals with normal color perception do not have to learn which colors are most readily nameable, because they come pre-equipped with an awareness of color salience. But they do have to learn how many of the salient colors are named in their language, and they must learn the particular labels their language gives to these colors. When devising ways to help people learn foreign languages, we have no need to teach the invariant aspects, and this makes Chomskian linguistics, with its emphasis on universals, an unlikely candidate for the most relevant linguistic theory for language pedagogy.

It is the variable component of language teachers must worry about, and its most obviously variable aspect is the lexicon. Measured by sheer information content—the bits of information we must hold somewhere in our heads if we are to communicate in the language—the lexicon certainly forms a considerable fraction of any language, and since the lexicon varies so markedly from one language to another, we can be certain that this large fraction has to be learned.

Conscious and Unconscious Aspects of Language

In the last chapter I suggested that the words of language can be distributed along a continuum that leads from the functional to the concrete. This continuum is related to, and is possibly a part of, an even broader continuum that reaches from the least conscious to the most conscious aspects of language.

Ordinary untutored speakers are far more aware of some aspects of their language than others, and at the most conscious extreme are their words, especially the most concrete words. People who lack any specialized training in language or linguistics sometimes act as if a language can be more or less fully accounted for by its dictionary. It is the words of the language that speakers can talk about easily, and it is the words that they are usually most interested in. We can define words for our children, and those of us who are literate can search out a word in the dictionary to find its pronunciation or meaning. We know that, from time to time, we continue to add to our stock of words.

This awareness of words may stem, in part, from our formal education. As we learn to read we are taught to recognize and talk about words, and we are given extensive instruction in the use of dictionaries. Even nonliterate people, however, have a far clearer idea of words and of their use than they have about any other aspect of their language. I once lived among a tribal people of northeastern India, many of whom were totally unschooled and unable to read even a single letter of the alphabet. They had trouble explaining anything about the phonology or grammar of their language to me, but they had no difficulty talking about words or defining them. When my language was still rudimentary, I would point to objects and ask for their names. Later, when I heard a more abstract term, I would stop the speaker and ask its meaning. No one had trouble helping me out. My questions seemed reasonable, and their answers were clear. Even these nonliterate people had a firm awareness of the words of their language, of the meaning of these words, and of how to help a foreigner understand and use them. Of course they were also skilled at using the grammar and phonology of their language, but they had very little ability to explain them and seemed hardly even aware of them.

At the opposite end from the lexicon, on the conscious to unconscious continuum, are the universal features that are built into all languages under the pressure of our inherited linguistic capacity. These aspects of language need never become conscious, precisely because they are built into us as part of our nature. Linguists have, in fact, been engaged in a long and difficult struggle, a struggle that is by no means completed, to try to discover the nature and extent of these universal features.

Somewhere between the conscious lexicon and the unconscious, innate, and universal constraints, we find other constraints—the grammatical patterns that are used by one language but not by others. The learned grammar—that aspect of grammar that varies from language to language—is manifested through the functional vocabulary that occupies the least concrete segment of the lexicon, and through the associated morphology. This learned but far from concrete aspect of language often lies outside our self-conscious awareness, until we work seriously to learn a foreign language. Only then do we discover that a language can be built along quite different principles from those we had always taken for granted. This part of a language can be brought into even fuller consciousness by more specialized study. Much of technical linguistics has amounted to a gradual expansion of our conscious knowledge about our ordinarily unconscious skills. For most monolingual speakers, however, much of the variable grammar remains largely unconscious, and even skilled bilinguals, especially those who learn both their languages in early childhood, seem to have no need for much conscious awareness of grammar.

These intermediate segments of language—variable rather than universal, but less conscious than the concrete lexicon—must be learned, but when they are learned in childhood, they develop almost outside the boundaries of consciousness. Children learn them without knowing that they are learning. This kind of learning is crucially important in human socialization, but it is a kind of learning for which our educational system is poorly equipped. It is in the nature of schools to focus on self-conscious learning. How in the world could schools teach things that students do not know they learn?

Adults can get some sense of how unconscious learning of the variable grammar can take place by working hard to understand a language without trying to speak it. Such adults soon discover that the kinds of grammatical rules students struggle with in conventional language classes are rarely needed and rarely even helpful. For a long period receptive learners will find that their comprehension is based largely on the recognition of individual, relatively content-full words. If they can understand enough of these full words, they will be able to make out the sense of a written passage or conversation, even though the functional words may remain murky and the morphology and syntax obscure. They will understand in the same way that the first passage on page 106 can be understood, as a sequence of understandable islands separated by somewhat distracting but not terribly relevant intervals of gibberish. Learners can deal with a sequence of words to which a semantic relationship can be assigned in spite of the lack of syntactic knowledge.

As comprehension improves, the islands of understanding slowly expand. Learners will find that the more functional words gradually come to be understood from being repeatedly encountered in context. They will also begin to recognize short phrases in addition to individual words. The juxtaposition of two familiar words will come to be readily understood when the pattern by which they are joined is a common one, even if the pattern itself is not self-consciously recognized. The ways in which the content words are arranged and the ways by which they change under varied circumstances will begin to seem natural, and it is this sense of naturalness that signals a growing knowledge of the grammar. For receptive foreign language learners, as for children, this sense of naturalness can be restricted to the borders of consciousness. It grows from hearing so many adjectives after so many nouns that this arrangement begins to seem like the only one possible. It comes from hearing *-ons* at the end of so many French verbs with *nous* as their subjects, that anything else would seem strange. This sense of the grammar emerges only gradually out of a vast experience with the language. We reverse the natural sequence when we start with even the minimal grammar that early learners need if they have to speak. Then we act as if grammar is a prerequisite to the experience of language. In effective language learning, grammar is not a prerequisite to experience, but its result.

Sounding Right

The sentence that the linguist describes as "grammatical" is said by others to "sound right," and there is a deep folk wisdom in this popular expression. "To be grammatical," and "to sound right" refer to much the same thing, but they put the emphasis in quite different places, for in spite of all denials, "grammaticality" is a term of production. We can talk about "speaking grammatically," but "hearing grammatically" makes no sense. Once again, the productive bias of so much linguistics, as of so much language pedagogy, is apparent.

To "sound right" shows a wonderful defiance of this productive bias, for by saying that something "sounds right" we shift our focus decisively to reception; we move the patterns of our language from our mouth to our ears. A sentence that "sounds right" fits patterns that have grown familiar by long exposure, and only when people have begun to have a sense of what sounds right are they in a position to start to talk. Only then can they effectively monitor their own speech. The only way to gain this sense of what sounds right is to have massive experience with right sounding language. This is not what we offer in most foreign language classrooms today. It is what we ought to offer if we want our students to learn.

Bibliography

Andersen, R.
    1979   Expanding Schumann's Pidginization Hypothesis. *Language Learning* 29:105–119.

Asher, James J.
    1966   The Learning Strategy of the Total Physical Response: A Review. *Modern Language Journal* 50:79–84.
    1969   The Total Physical Response Approach to Second Language Learning. *Modern Language Journal* 53:3–17.
    1972   Children's First Language as a Model for Second Language Learning. *Modern Language Journal* 56:133–139.
    1977   *Learning Another Language Through Actions. The Complete Teacher's Guide Book*. Los Gatos, Calif.: Sky Oaks Production.

Asher, James J., and R. Garcia
    1969   The Optimal Age to Learn a Foreign Language. *Modern Language Journal* 53:334–341.

Asher, James J., and B. S. Price
    1967   The Learning Strategy of the Total Physical Response: Some Age Differences. *Child Development* 38:1219–1227.

Asher, James J., J. Kasudo, and R. de la Torre
    1974   Learning a Second Language Through Commands: The Second Field Test. *Modern Language Journal* 58:24–32.

Atkinson, R. C.
    1975   Mnemotechnics in Second Language Learning. *American Psychologist* 30:821–828.

Ausubel, David P.
    1964   Adults Versus Children in Second Language Learning: Psychological Considerations. *The Modern Language Journal* 48:420–424.

Bailey, N., N. C. Madden, and S. Krashen
    1974   Is There a 'Natural Sequence' in Adult Second Language Learning? *Language Learning* 24:235–243.

Belasco, Simon
    1971a   C'est la guerre? or Can Cognition and Verbal Behavior Coexist? *Language and the Teacher*: A Series in Applied Linguistics, Vol. XVII: Toward a Cognitive Approach to Second Language Acquisition, ed. by Robert C. Lugton. Philadelphia: Center for Curriculum Development.
    1971b   The Feasibility of Learning a Second Language in an Artificial Unicultural Situation. In *The Psychology of Second Language Learning*, ed. by P. Pimsleur and T. Quinn, pp. 1–10. Cambridge, England: Cambridge University Press.

Berlin, Brent, and Paul Kay
    1969   *Basic Color Terms: Their Universality and Evolution*. Berkeley: University of California Press.

Bloom, Lois
 1974   Talking, Understanding, and Thinking. In *Language Perspectives—Acquisition, Retardation, and Intervention*, ed. by R. L. Schiefelbusch and L. L. Lloyd, pp. 285–311. Baltimore: University Park Press.
Brown, Gillian
 1977   *Listening to Spoken English*. London: Longman.
Brown, Roger, C. Cazden, and U. Bellugi
 1969   The Child's Grammar from I to III. In *Minnesota Symposia on Child Psychology*, Vol. 2, ed. by J. P. Hill. Minneapolis: University of Minnesota Press.
Burling, Robbins
 1965   *Hill Farms and Padi Fields*. Englewood Cliffs, N.J.: Prentice-Hall.
 1970   *Man's Many Voices*. New York: Holt, Rinehart and Winston.
 1978a   *Reading Français* (photocopied).
 1978b   An Introductory Course in Reading French. *Language Learning* 28:105–28.
 1980   Minimal Kommunikationsnivå i Svenska. *Hemspråk och svenska* 80(4):26–31.
 1981   Social Constraints on Adult Language Learning. In *Native Language and Foreign Language Acquisition*, ed. by Harris Winitz. Annals of the New York Academy of Sciences. New York: NYAS.
Burling, Robbins, and A. L. Becker
 1979   Machine Aided Instruction in Aural Comprehension of Indonesian. Final Report. ERIC ED 195–134.
Burling, Robbins, A. L. Becker, P. B. Henry, and J. N. Tomasowa
 1981   Machine Aided Instruction in Bahasa Indonesia. In *The Comprehension Approach to Foreign Language Instruction*, ed. by Harris Winitz, pp. 154–169. Rowley, Mass.: Newbury House.
Chapman, Robin S.
 1974   Developmental Relationship Between Receptive and Expressive Language. In *Language Perspectives—Acquisition, Retardation, and Intervention*, ed. by R. L. Schiefelbusch and L. L. Lloyd, pp. 335–344. Baltimore: University Park Press.
Chastain, Kenneth
 1976   *Developing Second-Language Skills: Theory to Practice*, Second Edition. Chicago: Rand McNally.
Chomsky, Noam
 1965   *Aspects of the Theory of Syntax*. Cambridge, Mass.: M.I.T. Press.
 1968   *Language and Mind*. New York: Harcourt Brace Jovanovich.
 1969   Linguistics and Philosophy. In *Language and Philosophy*, ed. by Sidney Hook, pp. 52–94. New York: New York University Press.
Clark, Ruth
 1974   Performing Without Competence. *Journal of Child Language* 1(1):1–10.
Clark, Ruth, Sandy Hutcheson, and Paul Van Buren
 1974   Comprehension and Production in Language Acquisition. *Journal of Linguistics* 10:39–54.
Close, R. A.
 1977   Banners and Bandwagons. *E.L.I. Journal* 30(3):175–183.

Corder, S. P.
1967   The Significance of Learners' Errors. *International Review of Applied Linguistics* (5):161–169.

Curtiss, Susan
1977   *Genie: A Psycholinguistic Study of Modern-Day "Wild Child."* New York: Academic Press.

Daudet, Alphonse
1910   La derniere classe. In *Contes Choisis: La Fantaisie et L'histoire.* Paris: E. Fasquelle.

Davies, Norman F.
1976   Receptive Versus Productive Skills in Foreign Language Learning. *Modern Language Journal* 60:440–443.
1980   Putting Receptive Skills First: An Experiment in Sequencing. *Canadian Modern Language Review* 36(3):461–467.

Deveny, John J., and J. C. Bookout
1976   The Intensive Language Course: Toward a Successful Approach. *Foreign Language Annals,* pp. 58–64.

Dulay, Heidi C., and Marina K. Burt
1974   Natural Sequences in Child Second Language Acquisition. *Language Learning* 24(1):37–53.
1978   Some Remarks on Creativity in Language Acquisition. In *Second Language Acquisition Research: Issues and Implications,* ed. by W. C. Ritchie. New York: Academic Press.

Ehrmann, Eliezer L.
1963   Listening Comprehension in the Teaching of a Foreign Language. *Modern Language Journal* 47:18–20.

Ervin-Tripp, Susan
1971   An Overview of Theories of Grammatical Development. In *The Ontogenesis of Grammar,* ed. by D. E. Slobin. New York and London: Academic Press.
1974   Is Second Language Learning Like the First? *TESOL Quarterly* 8(2):111–127.

Fahmy, Nermine
1979   An Investigation of the Effectiveness of Extensive Listening and Reading Practice on Students' Ability to Read English. Master's thesis. Cairo: American University of Cairo.

Ferguson, Charles A.
1971   Absence of Copula and the Notion of Simplicity: A Study of Normal Speech, Baby Talk, Foreigner Talk and Pidgins. In *Pidginization and Creolization of Languages,* ed. by D. Hymes. Cambridge, England: Cambridge University Press.
1975   Toward a Characterization of English Foreigner Talk. *Anthropological Linguistics* 17(1):1–14.

Freed, Barbara F.
1980   Talking to Foreigners Versus Talking to Children: Similarities and Differences. In *Los Angeles Second Language Acquisition Research Forum* (2nd), ed. by R. C. Scarcella and S. D. Krashen. Rowley, Mass.: Newbury House.

Fries, Charles C.
1945   *Teaching and Learning English as a Foreign Language.* Ann Arbor:
          University of Michigan Press.
Gary, Judith O.
1974   The Effects on Children of Delayed Oral Practice in Initial Stages of
          Second Language Learning. Ph.D. dissertation. Los Angeles:
          U.C.L.A.
1975   Delayed Oral Practice in Initial Stages of Second Language
          Learning. In *New Directions in Second Language Teaching and
          Bilingual Education,* ed. by Marina K. Burt and Heidi C. Dulay.
          Washington, D.C.: TESOL.
1978   Why Talk If You Don't Have To? In *Second Language Acquisition
          Research: Issues and Implications,* ed. by W. C. Ritchie. New York:
          Academic Press.
Gary, Judith O., and Norman Gary
1980   Comprehension-Oriented Foreign Language Instruction—An
          Overview. *The Linguistic Reporter* 23(3):4–5.
1981   Caution: Talking May Be Dangerous to Your Linguistic Health! The
          Case for a Much Greater Emphasis on Listening Comprehension in
          Foreign Language Instruction. *International Review of Applied
          Linguistics* 19.
Hammond, Sandra B., and C. Edward Scebold
1980   Survey of Foreign Language Enrollments in Public Secondary
          Schools, Fall 1978. Final Report, Grant No. G 00701693. Office of
          International Education, U.S. Department of Education.
Hanania, Edith A. S.
1974   Acquisition of English Structures: A Case Study of an Adult Native
          Speaker of Arabic in an English-Speaking Environment. Ph.D.
          dissertation. Bloomington: Indiana University.
Hanania, Edith A. S., and Harry L. Gradman
1977   Acquisition of English Structures: A Case Study of an Adult Native
          Speaker of Arabic in an English-Speaking Environment. *Language
          Learning* 27:75–91.
Harris, Julian, and André Lévêque
1973   *Basic Conversational French.* New York: Holt, Rinehart and
          Winston.
Hatch, Evelyn Marcussen (ed.)
1978   *Second Language Acquisition.* Rowley, Mass.: Newbury House.
Hill, Jane
1970   Foreign Accents, Language Acquisition and Cerebral Dominance
          Revisited. *Language Learning* 20:237–248.
Ingram, David
1974   The Relationship Between Comprehension and Production. In
          *Language Perspectives—Acquisition, Retardation, and Interven-
          tion,* ed. by R. L. Schiefelbusch and L. L. Lloyd, pp. 313–334.
          Baltimore: University Park Press.
Ingram, Frank, J. R. Nord, and D. Dragt
1975   A Program for Listening Comprehension. *Slavic and East European
          Journal* 19:1–10.

Jespersen, Otto
1904   *How to Teach a Foreign Language.* New York: Macmillan.
Kay, Paul, and Chad K. McDaniel
1978   The Linguistic Significance of the Meanings of Basic Color Terms. *Language* 54(3):610–646.
Kelly, L. G.
1969   *25 Centuries of Language Teaching.* Rowley, Mass.: Newbury House.
Krashen, Stephen D.
1973   Lateralization, Language Learning and the Critical Period: Some New Evidence. *Language Learning* 23:63–74.
1975   The Critical Period for Language Acquisition and Its Possible Bases. In *Developmental Psycholinguistics and Communication Disorders*, ed. by D. Aaronson and R. W. Reiber. Annals of the New York Academy of Sciences. New York: NYAS. 211–224.
1976   Formal and Informal Linguistic Environments in Language Learning and Language Acquisition. *TESOL Quarterly* 10:157–168.
1977   Some Issues Relating to the Monitor Model. In *On TESOL '77*, ed. by H. Brown, C. Yorio, and R. Crymes, pp. 144–158. Washington, D.C.: TESOL.
1979   Adult Second Language Acquisition as Post Critical Period Learning. *ITL, Review of Applied Linguistics* 43:39–52.
1981   The Input Hypothesis. In *Georgetown University Round Table on Languages and Linguistics, 1980*, ed. by James E. Alatis, pp. 168–180. Washington, D.C.: Georgetown University Press.
Krashen, Stephen, C. Jones, S. Zelinski, and C. Usprich
1978   How Important Is Instruction? *English Language Teaching Journal* 32(4):257–261.
Krashen, Stephen D., M. A. Lang, and R. C. Scarcella
1979   Age, Rate and Eventual Attainment in Second Language Acquisition. *TESOL Quarterly* 13(4):573–582.
Kučera, Henry, and W. Nelson Francis
1967   *Computational Analysis of Present-Day American English.* Providence, R.I.: Brown University Press.
Lamendella, John T.
1977   General Principles of Neurofunctional Organization and Their Manifestation in Primary and Nonprimary Language Acquisition. *Language Learning* 27:155–196.
Leech, Geoffrey, and Jan Svartvik
1975   *A Communicative Grammar of English.* London: Longman.
Lenneberg, E. H.
1962   Understanding Language Without Ability to Speak: A Case Report. *Journal of Abnormal and Social Psychology* 65:419–425.
1967   *Biological Foundations of Language.* New York: Wiley.
Leopold, W. F.
1954   A Child's Learning of Two Languages. *Georgetown University Round Table on Languages and Linguistics* 7:19–30. Washington, D.C.: Georgetown University Press.

Levin, Joel R.
1979   Assessing the Classroom Potential of the Keyword Method. *Journal of Educational Psychology* 71:583–594.
Macnamara, J.
1972   Cognitive Basis of Language Learning in Infants. *Psychology Review* 79:1–13.
MacNeilage, Peter F., T. P. Rootes, and C. R. Allen
1967   Speech Production and Perception in a Patient With Severe Impairment of Somesthetic Perception and Motor Control. *Journal of Speech and Hearing Research* 10:449–467.
Majhanovic, Suzanne
1979   Training the Ear: Listening Exercises for the Classroom. *Canadian Modern Language Review* 35:661–672.
Mason, C.
1971   The Relevance of Intensive Training in English as a Foreign Language for University Students. *Language Learning* 21:197–201.
McNeill, D.
1970   *The Acquisition of Language: The Study of Developmental Psycholinguistics.* New York: Harper & Row.
Merry, R.
1980   The Keyword Method and Children's Vocabulary Learning in the Classroom. *British Journal of Educational Psychology* 50(2):23–36.
Morley, Joan
1972   *Improving Aural Comprehension.* Ann Arbor: University of Michigan Press.
1976   *Listening Dictation.* Ann Arbor: University of Michigan Press.
Morrison, Scott E.
1977   Foreign Language Enrollments in U.S. Colleges and Universities— Fall 1977. New York: Modern Language Association.
Myklebust, H. R.
1957   *Auditory Disorders in Children.* New York: Grune and Stratton.
Neufeld, Gerald G.
1979   Towards a Theory of Language Learning Ability. *Language Learning* 29:227–241.
1980   On the Adult's Ability to Acquire Phonology. *TESOL Quarterly* 14:285–298.
Newmark, Leonard
1966   How Not to Interfere with Language Learning. In *Language Learning: The Individual and the Process,* International Journal of American Linguistics, Publication 40, Vol. 32, No. 1 (Jan. 1966):77–83.
1971   A Minimal Language-Teaching Program. In *The Psychology of Second Language Learning,* ed. by P. Pimsleur and T. Quinn, pp. 11–18. Cambridge, England: Cambridge University Press.
Nida, Eugene A.
1971   Mastery Learning and Foreign Languages. In *The Psychology of Second Language Learning,* ed. by P. Pimsleur and T. Quinn, pp. 67–73. Cambridge, England: Cambridge University Press.
Nord, James R.
1980   Developing Listening Fluency Before Speaking: An Alternative Paradigm. *System* 8:1–22.

Oller, John W., Jr.
1971   Language Communication and Second Language Learning. In *The Psychology of Second Language Learning*, ed. by P. Pimsleur and T. Quinn, pp. 171–179. Cambridge, England: Cambridge University Press.

Oller, John W., Jr., and N. Nagato
1974   The Long Term Effect of FLES. *Modern Language Journal* 58:15–19.

Ott, C. E., D. C. Butler, Q. S. Blake, and J. P. Ball
1973   The Effect of Interactive-Image Elaboration on the Acquisition of Foreign Language Vocabulary. *Language Learning* 73:197–206.

Palmer, Harold E.
1968   *The Scientific Study and Teaching of Languages* (orig. pub. 1917). London: Oxford Press.

Penfield, W., and L. Roberts
1959   *Speech and Brain Mechanisms*. Princeton, N.J.: Princeton University Press.

Pike, Kenneth L.
1967   *Language in Relation to a Unified Theory of the Structure of Human Behavior*. The Hague: Mouton.

Pimsleur, Paul, and Terence Quinn
1971   *The Psychology of Second Language Learning*. Cambridge, England: Cambridge University Press.

Politzer, Robert L., Michio P. Hagiwara, and Jean R. Carduner
1966   *L'Échelle*. Waltham, Mass.: Blaisdell.

Politzer, Robert L., and Charles N. Staubach
1961   *Teaching Spanish: A Linguistic Orientation*. Boston: Ginn.

Postovsky, Valerian A.
1970   Effects of Delay in Oral Practice at the Beginning of Second Language Learning. Ph.D. dissertation. Berkeley: University of California.

1974   Effects of Delay in Oral Practice at the Beginning of Second Language Learning. *Modern Language Journal* 58(5–6):229–239.

1975a   On Paradoxes in Foreign Language Teaching. *Modern Language Journal* 59:18–21.

1975b   The Priority of Aural Comprehension in the Language Acquisition Process. Paper delivered at the 4th AILA World Congress, Stuttgart.

1977   Why Not Start Speaking Later? In *Viewpoints on English as a Second Language*, ed. by M. Burt, H. Dulay, and M. Finocchario. New York: Regents.

Quirk, Randolf, Sidney Greenbaum, Geoffrey Leech, and Jan Svartvik
1972   *A Grammar of Contemporary English*. New York: Seminar Press.

Reeds, James A., Harris Winitz, and Paul A. García
1977   A Test of Reading Following Comprehension Training. *International Review of Applied Linguistics in Language Teaching* 15:307–319.

Richards, Jack C.
1973   Error Analysis and Second Language Strategies. In *Focus on the Learner: Pragmatic Perspectives for the Language Teacher*, ed. by J. W. Oller and J. C. Richards. Rowley, Mass.: Newbury House.

Ritchie, William C. (ed.)
1978   *Second Language Acquisition Research: Issues and Implications.*
          New York: Academic Press.
Schaefer, Halmuth H.
1963   A Vocabulary Program Using "Language Redundancy." *Journal of
          Programmed Instruction* 2:9–16.
Scherer, George A. C.
1950   The Psychology of Teaching Reading through Listening. *German
          Quarterly* 23:151–160.
1952   The Importance of Auditory Comprehension. *German Quarterly*
          25:223–229.
Schiefelbusch, Richard C., and Lyle L. Lloyd
1974   *Language Perspectives—Acquisition, Retardation, and Interven-
          tion.* Baltimore: University Park Press.
Schlesinger, I. M.
1968   *Sentence Structure and the Reading Process.* The Hague and Paris:
          Mouton.
Schumann, John H.
1978a   *The Pidginization Process.* Rowley, Mass.: Newbury House.
1978b   The Relationship of Pidginization, Creolization and Decreolization
          to Second Language Acquisition. *Language Learning* 28:367–379.
Schumann, John H., and Nancy Stenson (eds.)
1974   *New Frontiers in Second Language Learning.* Rowley, Mass.:
          Newbury House.
Scovel, Thomas
1969   Foreign Accents, Language Acquistion and Cerebral Dominance.
          Language Learning 19:245–254.
Seliger, Herbert W.
1978   Implications of a Multiple Critical Periods Hypothesis for Second
          Language Learning. In *Second Language Acquisition Research:
          Issues and Implications,* ed. by W. C. Ritchie. New York: Academic
          Press.
Selinker, Larry
1972   Interlanguage. *International Review of Applied Linguistics in
          Language Teaching* 10:209–231.
Selinker, Larry, M. Swain, and G. Dumas
1975   The Interlanguage Hypothesis Extended to Children *Language
          Learning* 25:139–152.
Shapira, Rina G.
1978   The Non-Learning of English: Case Study of an Adult. In *Second
          Language Acquisition,* ed. by Evelyn Marcussen Hatch, pp. 246–255.
          Rowley, Mass.: Newbury House.
Simenon, Georges
1971   *Le Meurtre d'un Etudiant,* ed. by Frédéric Ernst. New York: Holt,
          Rinehart and Winston.
Skutnabb-Kangas, Tove, and P. Toukomaa
1976   Teaching Migrant Children's Mother Tongue and Learning the
          Language of the Host Country in the Context of the Socio-Cultural
          Situation of the Migrant Family. *Tutkimuksia Research Reports*
          (15). Department of Sociology and Social Psychology, University of
          Tampere, Finland.

Slobin, Dan I.
1971   *The Ontogenesis of Grammar*. New York: Academic Press.
1975   On the Nature of Talk to Children. In *Foundations of Language Development: A Multidisciplinary Approach*, Vol. I, ed. by E. H. Lenneberg and E. Lenneberg, pp. 283–297. New York: Academic Press.

Snow, Becky G., and Kyle Perkins
1979   The Teaching of Listening Comprehension and Communication Activities. *TESOL Quarterly* 13(1):51–63.

Snow, Catherine E., and Charles A. Ferguson
1977   *Talking to Children*. Cambridge, England: Cambridge University Press.

Snow, Catherine E., and Marian Hoefnagel-Höhle
1977   Age Differences in Pronunciation of Foreign Sounds. *Language and Speech* 20:357–365.
1978   Age Differences in Second Language Acquisition. In *Second Language Acquisition*, ed. Evelyn Marcussen Hatch. Rowley, Mass.: Newbury House.

Sorenson, Arthur P.
1967   Multilingualism in the Northwest Amazon. *American Anthropologist* 69:670–684.

Stanley, J.
1978   Teaching Listening Comprehension: An Interim Report on a Project to Use Uncontrolled Language Data as a Source Material for Training Foreign Students in Listening Comprehension. *TESOL Quarterly* 12:285–295.

Storer, Mary E. (ed.)
1952   *Les Jeux Sont Faits*, by Jean-Paul Sartre. Englewood Cliffs, N.J.: Prentice-Hall.

Strevens, Peter
1977   *New Orientations in the Teaching of English*. Oxford, England: Oxford University Press.

Swaffar, Janet King, and Margaret S. Woodruff
1978   Language for Comprehension: Focus on Reading. A Report on the University of Texas German Program. *Modern Language Journal* 62(1–2):27–32.

Sweet, Henry
1964   *The Practical Study of Languages; A Guide for Teachers and Learners*. London: Oxford University Press. (First published in 1899.)

Tongue, R. K.
n.d.   Reading Bahasa Indonesia for English-Speaking Students of Language (Mimeographed).

Upshur, J.
1968   Four Experiments in the Relation Between Foreign Language Teaching and Learning. *Language Learning*, 18:111–124.

Wagner-Gough, Judy, and E. M. Hatch
1975   The Importance of Input Data in Second Language Acquisition Studies. *Language Learning* 25:297–308.

Wardhaugh, Ronald
    1974   The Contrastive Analysis Hypothesis. In *New Frontiers in Second Language Learning*, ed. by John H. Schumann and Nancy Stenson, pp. 13–18. Rowley, Mass.: Newbury House.
Whitaker, Harry A.
    1978   Bilingualism: A Neurolinguistics Perspective. In *Second Language Acquisition Research: Issues and Implications*, ed. by W. C. Ritchie, pp. 21–32. New York: Academic Press.
Wilkins, David A.
    1972a   *Linguistics in Language Teaching*. Cambridge, Mass.: M.I.T. Press.
    1972b   Grammatical, Situational and Notional Syllabuses. In *Proceedings of the Third International Congress of Applied Linguistics*, Copenhagen, Vol. II, pp. 254–265.
    1976   *Notional Syllabuses*. Oxford, England: Oxford University Press.
Winitz, Harris
    1973   Problem Solving and the Delaying of Speech as Strategies in the Teaching of Language. *American Speech and Hearing Association* 15(10):586.
    1981a   *The Comprehension Approach to Foreign Language Instruction*. Rowley, Mass.: Newbury House.
    1981b   A Reconsideration of Comprehension and Production in Language Training. In Winitz, 1981a, pp. 101–140.
    1981c   *Native Language and Foreign Language Acquisition*. Annals of the New York Academic of Sciences. New York: NYAS.
Winitz, Harris, and J. A. Reeds
    1973   Rapid Acquisition of a Foreign Language (German) by the Avoidance of Speaking. *IRAL* 11:295–317.
    1975   *Comprehension and Problem Solving as Strategies for Language Training*. The Hague: Mouton.
Wolski, W.
    1962   Language Development of Normal Children Four, Five, and Six Years of Age as Measured by the Michigan Picture Language Inventory. Ph.D. dissertation. Ann Arbor: University of Michigan.

Index